'DELIGHTFULLY IMPERFECT'

After thirteen visits to Sri Lanka, Paul Harris, an award-winning international journalist and author of more than forty books, decided to make his home on the Indian Ocean sunshine island he had come to love. He would be there for a year, working for *The Daily Telegraph* and *Janes Intelligence Review*. He stayed most of the time at the renowned Galle Face Hotel, the oldest hotel in the world east of Suez, before being personally expelled by Prime Minister Ranil Wickremesinghe on an ultimatum from the rebel Tamil Tigers (LTTE). This is the story of a remarkable year at the Galle Face Hotel. It not only paints a fascinating inside picture of a legendary hotel, but it also provides a unique perspective on politics and conflict in a beautiful but troubled tropical island.

The Galle Face Hotel

N 06 55'17".8
E 079 50'74".1

'DELIGHTFULLY IMPERFECT'
A Year in Sri Lanka
at The Galle Face Hotel

Paul Harris

Line drawings & cover by
Sanjeewee Seneviratne

Best wishes
Paul Harris
(& Lucy)
December 2014

K&B

Published by
Kennedy and Boyd
an imprint of
Zeticula
57 St Vincent Crescent
Glasgow
G3 8NQ
Scotland, U.K.

http://www.kennedyandboyd.co.uk
admin@kennedyandboyd.co.uk

ISBN 1-904999-38-7 Paperback
ISBN 978-1-904999-38-6 Paperback

Contents

Balcony suites, study.

Introduction

I remember when the confirmation of my first reservation at the Galle Face Hotel emerged from the fax machine. It was back in December of 1995 in the full, uncompromising chill of a Scottish winter. A pen and ink representation of palm trees and a grandiose colonial-style building suggested exciting exotica well beyond the misty horizons of the snow-capped Lammermuir Hills, outside my rain-spattered office window. The promise of a warm welcome was instantly communicated by the letterhead confirming the reservation: 'Established 1864. Dedicated to Yesterday's Charm and Tomorrow's Comfort'. The yesterday's charm bit would prove wholly accurate as a claim. Tomorrow's comfort, well . . .

The text of the confirmation for my stay in the oldest hotel in the world, east of Suez, also augured well. My journalist's letterhead had prompted an unexpected – quite unprecedented - offer. A ten per cent 'writer's discount' seemed admirably quaint; and an upgrade to a de-luxe room was laudably generous. I had, of course, heard talk of this place from friends, and also read in guide books about the well-nigh legendary Galle Face Hotel. One writer, aptly as it would turn out, had referred to the hotel as 'a colonial time machine'. I came to realise that it must surely be a unique survival in a world of tens of thousands of sanitised, box-like hotels boasting every imaginable – and some unimaginable – facilities.

The oldest hotel east of Suez was founded in 1864: twelve years before the Bangkok Oriental opened its doors; 46 years before Singapore's Raffles Hotel (1910) and predating the Imperial in Tokyo (1890), the Taj Mahal in Bombay (1903), the Manila Hotel (1912) and the Hong Kong Peninsula (1928): and 23 years before the upstart Conrad Hilton was even born. Just in case you forget that last point, there is plaque in the hotel recording it for posterity. There are many sobriquets applied to the hotel known to its intimates as simply the 'GFH': Asia's Emerald on the Green, the Grande Dame of Serendip and The Beautiful Duchess are but a few.

In so many ways, The Galle Face Hotel is a mirror to the rest of what was once Ceylon, now known as Sri Lanka. Over the years, developments and events centred around the hotel have, to a very large extent, reflected those throughout the island as a whole. And, like Sri Lanka more generally, the GFH is 'delightfully imperfect', to quote from its erstwhile owner, the late Cyril Gardiner.

Almost six years after my first visit to Sri Lanka and the Galle Face Hotel, I decided, after thirteen visits to the country I had grown to love, to attempt to settle down there. I had felt so much at home in Sri Lanka that I was baffled by an intangible sensation of having found myself at home. And so, at the beginning of November 2001, I vacated my home in an 88-roomed mansion in Scotland, leased it out, packed a few possessions into two suitcases, and flew to Sri Lanka. With nowhere to live on a more permanent basis, I booked myself into a suite in the Galle Face Hotel overlooking the Indian Ocean.

It was, for me, the beginning of an idyll. Alas, it was not to last. This is the story of one year in Sri Lanka . . .

Oldest East of Suez

It is known to its fans simply as the 'GFH'. In its full, extended version the name Galle Face Hotel is pronounced as in ancient 'Gaul'. Somehow the GFH contrived to survive the depredations of the 20th century which so marred Ceylon, now Sri Lanka: wars, riots, insurrection and bomb attacks. At the beginning of the 21st century, its vast colonial pile resolutely survives, facing defiantly onto the Galle Face Green and the rather more vulgar modern, downtown Colombo.

The name Galle Face was given by the English colonialists to the gate of the Portuguese colonialists' Santa Cruz fortress in Colombo. It faced towards the commercially important port of Galle on the south coast of old Ceylon. Not all historians agree, however, on this explanation of the origin of the name. The mid-19th century British civil servant and writer James Tennent ascribed it, instead, to the Dutch word *faas*, which means the front – or the face – of the fortifications of the Fort district, which, in turn, faced towards Galle. The very oldest Dutch map of Colombo bears a reference to a *fausse bray*, or ditch and parapet military fortification. It is known that the Dutch called the South Gate in their fortifications the 'Gale Gate', so it is entirely possible that they termed their fortifications the 'Gale Faas'.

The Green was effectively encircled to the north east by the Beira Lake, named after the Dutch water engineer De Beira; to the north by the old Colombo Fort and ramparts built on drained marshes; and to the south by the Hotel. Until September 1833, execution by firing squad was still conducted on the Green and the armies of successive invaders – Portuguese, Dutch and British – drilled on its grass in close proximity to the old barracks which stood on the site of the present Galadari Hotel. During the 19th century, however, it gradually became popular for the more peaceful pursuits of promenading, horse riding and enjoying the sea air in open carriage. In those early days of colonial rule, the island's new masters lived either behind the ramparts of the Fort district or along the bustling streets of Pettah. Daily escape to the Galle Face Green was something of a necessity for physical and mental health. Of a morning there was the fresh sea air to be enjoyed; of an evening, the spectacular sunsets. The Green came to be referred to as 'the lungs of Colombo'. In those days it was a vast area but the passage of years has seen it gradually encroached upon by road and hotel development and, indeed, by the present headquarters of the army and the Ministry of Defence, and these days it is down to a relatively paltry 18 acres.

In the early 1820s the value of the Galle Face Green was officially recognised. Sir Edward Barnes, then Lieutenant Governor of the island, was a keen horse racing chap. He discerned that this vast open space would make a splendid racecourse and the first of many modifications were made to the Green. The area to be used for the track was levelled and re-turfed; the untidy and unsuitable raised section on the sea side was cleared and centuries of damage caused by termites and land crabs was repaired. The first 'Race Meet', as it was termed, was held in 1821 on what came to be known as the Colpetty Racecourse. The course was a mile and a quarter in length and its starting point in those days was an old colonial villa built in the days of the Dutch. It can be seen in contemporary paintings, large and grand and set against a backdrop of trees at the very southern end of the Green. Fifty years later, this would become the first home of the present Galle Face Hotel.

The racecourse firmly established the social *cachet* of the Green. As the Colombo Journal reported, 'a more splendid assemblage is rarely to be found in any society than that we have witnessed on the Colombo Racecourse.' Ten or more years later, a new structure took shape near the middle of the track: a building described at the time as being of 'the nightcap order of architecture'. A circular building with a thatched roof, *cadjan* in local parlance, this would variously be known as the pavilion, grandstand or race bungalow. Over the years it would be much improved, added to and rendered altogether more permanent until it resembled the structure we still see remaining before the modern Taj Samudra Hotel. A larger version of the surviving structure was opened as a full grandstand in September 1870 by the incorporated Assembly Rooms Company Limited.

By the mid 19th century, the Green was not quite yet at the height of its popularity and prestige. H C Sirr, Deputy Queen's Advocate, observed in 1850 that 'about half past five o'clock, the Galle Face, or Hyde Park of Colombo, begins to wear an animated appearance, there being many vehicles and horses in motion. Every description of conveyance is seen driving around the Galle Face from the Long Acre [London] built carriage of the Governor and the dashing phaeton of the wealthy merchant, to the uncanny gig, the country built palanquin and the humble bandy.'

But in 1856, British Governor Sir Henry Ward commenced formal development of the Green as a place of recreation, creating a place to walk along the seashore amidst the carriages. He decreed that the Green should in future exist for the pleasure and recreation of the people of Colombo and when work was completed in 1859 there was a stone plaque which sternly recommended it 'to his successors in the interests of the Ladies and Children of Colombo'.

In 1880, the visiting German scientist, Ernest Haeckel, notes 'the gilded youth of Colombo exhibit themselves on horseback, some of them on miserable hacks indeed, [whilst] the ladies with bouquets in their hands, recline languidly in their carriages in the highest and most elegant *toilettes*. But no sooner is the sun gone down [than] they all hasten home; partly in order to escape the fever-laden evening air, partly to go through an elaborate process of "dressing for dinner", which is usually at half-past seven, and of course in the indispensable black tail-coat and white neck-tie, as in "Old England".'

The editor of *The Times of Ceylon* observed about this time what would become an enduring feature of the Green. 'It is doubtful whether even the drawing rooms of public assemblies are more frequently the birthplace of love between youthful members of Colombo society than the Galle Face green. Certain is it that many chose the lovely ride and the confidential friendship that it engenders for the disclosure and making of what is vulgarly called a proposal ...'.

The Galle Face Hotel was conceived and incorporated as a hotel – The Ceylon Hotels Company Ltd – in February 1864. Several notable local businessmen were involved including George Wall, H C Buchanan and H Thomas. A working capital of fifty thousand pounds sterling was authorised in the company's articles and there was a share issue at ten pounds a share: a considerable sum in those far off days. The shares were not fully subscribed but the company was able to acquire three properties, one of which was on the southern end of Galle Face Green. An extremely rough and ready hostelry on a two acre site was located in the form of Galle Face House, the large villa built by a former Dutch colonialist and purchased by the directors of Ceylon Hotels in 1871. The house is depicted in several paintings and prints and an old photograph survives which shows horses and riders ready for the off at the Starter's Gate with the building behind. It appears that the large main drawing room was located in the centre; an arch led through to the dining room and the bedrooms were spread out on the wings on either side. Outhouses contained store rooms, servants' quarters, kitchens and other domestic offices. In those days it was not the prestigious hotel that it would later become. It was more of a transit lodge for planters and others in town from up country before they joined a ship at the harbour. A traveller by the name of Hugh Blacklaw describes two places he overnighted in: The Galle Face Hotel and the Royal in the Fort. He is notably uncomplimentary about the Galle Face:

'There was a shanty called the Galle Face Hotel, where the modern one of that name stands today. They were both paragons of dirt. The Galle Face Hotel was the sort of place you get away from as soon as possible, it was so bad. No privacy, no cleanliness, canvas partitions and dirt – worse than any fifth rate place you see in some towns now . . .' Edward Lear, of limerick fame, was equally uncomplimentary about the original Galle Face Hotel and also applied his caustic pen to the establishment.

It is recorded that the house had enjoyed a lucky survival in the 1840s when British military cannon practice went awry. A cannonball misfired on a particularly wild monsoon day and all 30 pounds of it were drawn by the wind almost a mile down the Green to score a direct hit on the roof of the villa where it landed on 'the squared *chunam* and terracotta tiled floor leaving a heavy dent, where it rolled under a chair and remained.' [Deloraine Brohier in *The Saga of the Colombo Club*]. When he heard of the incident, Governor Sir Colin Campbell arrived to view 'the incredible cannon ball'.

In early summer of the same year of 1871 another landmark on the Galle Face esplanade was inaugurated with the opening of the Colombo Club in the Race Bungalow, leased from the Assembly Rooms Company Limited. An article entitled 'Old Coaching Days' [*The Sunday Illustrated*, May 24 1924] looks back at the founding of the Club and expresses the view that it came into existence on account of 'the smallness of the GFH' and its inability to serve the increased demands for accommodation in Colombo. The club has since moved on but its original antique, curious oval-shaped home still remains at the front of the Taj Samudra. The urban sprawl of Colombo had yet to spread south beyond Galle Face Green. But the expansion of the city and its infrastructure was already on the way. In1876, work was commenced on the railway line from Colombo to Galle, threatening to rudely intrude upon the hotel's uninterrupted access to the sea. The Directors of the hotel successfully lobbied for the line to skirt their gardens and preserved their position as the operators of Colombo's only seaside hotel.

In 1887, the Golden Jubilee of Queen Victoria was celebrated in front of the site of the hotel that would newly rise on the Green. *The Ceylon Examiner* reported, 'Never before did Galle Face Green look prettier and never did so large an assemblage gather on it.' It was said that more than 20,000 people gathered and, from a specially constructed pavilion, Governor Sir Arthur Gordon read a somewhat wordy account of Her Majesty's reign which, by all accounts, succeeded in boring the most avid Royalists. This was also read out in Tamil and Sinhala and it was evening time before those gathered were treated to long awaited fireworks.

These were, quite simply, the most extravagant days of the British Empire: unchallenged and supreme, it straddled the world, its power and omnipotence without equal, its values and social ranking the unquestioned order of the day. When the American Mary Thorn Carpenter visited Colombo she noted that in the hotel all the servants were men. There was but one form of address for them, old or young, and that was 'boy'. It seemed absurd to an egalitarian, democratic American to have to call a grave, white-bearded man 'boy'.

The present three-storied hotel building was fully completed in 1894 in what the hotel itself expansively describes as 'grand renaissance style', replacing the old Galle Face House which was demolished. In those days, most of the grand residences of the Europeans were still in the Fort. Development had not yet moved out down the Galle Road. Accordingly, there was ample space for a grand and sprawling hotel building. The new hotel building took the form of a long, three-storied central block, flanked by four-storey pavilions at either end, and a matching roofed portico placed in the centre. The architect was one E Skinner, who also designed the Grand Oriental Hotel, and the hotel was constructed by the Muslim building contractor, A M Wapchi Marikar.

Marikar, a master mason turned contractor, was the leading builder in Colombo around the turn of the century. Apart from the Hotel, he also built the best of the colonial edifices: the General Post Office, the Colombo Museum, the Clock Tower, the Old Town Hall in Pettah, the Customs Building and the Finlay Moir Building.

Photographs taken at the turn of the 19th century depict the Galle Face Hotel in its grand colonial heyday. The stonework is pristine and unpainted, there is a profusion of palms at the front of the building and the lawns are graced by elegant rattan furniture. In those days, a band played twice a week against the backdrop of the Indian Ocean as the sun set red on the sea. One photograph shows the 'dining hall' with tables and chairs sufficient for 350 diners: the largest dining room on the island and, said some, east of Suez.

The public rooms in the building constructed in 1894 were singularly impressive even by the grandiose standards of the British Empire. The dining hall was 76 feet long, 39 feet wide and 30 feet high: the largest hall of any type on the island. The building accommodated the only swimming pool on the island – then generously sized at 50 by 20 foot - and there was an impressive Empire-style ballroom. The ballroom was of a similar grand size and was home to the Race Ball every August and the New Year's Eve Fancy Dress Ball. A second ballroom was created later with a Roman-style dome shaped ceiling draped in red cloth.

The drawing room boasted a Bechstein Grand piano and the 60 foot by 39 foot public billiard room four Burroughs & Watts tables. There was also a smaller private billiard room for ladies. The Burma teak panelled reading room and library (now the Chairman's office) had the best selection of current magazines on the island and there was a saloon bar size 52 by 36 foot which was 'stocked with specially imported wines, spirits and cigars – with all, in fact, that a thirsty yet fastidious man may require.' The first case of Pimms ever exported was sent to the new hotel. The whole was well set off by the wide, generous verandas, the terraced gardens sloping gently down to the sea, and the lofty, colonnaded reception hall. On a distinctly practical note, it was the first hotel in Ceylon to utilise gas for lighting and cooking and there was a wood-panelled lift which is now something of an antique but is still in use.

Alterations and renovations have been made to the original structure over the years, the most significant being the addition of the south wing in 1920 and staircase and other alterations in 1976. In 2002 work was recommenced on the south wing, abandoned in 1980, and which has been completely refurbished in the fashionable international, so-called 'boutique' hotel style with Jacuzzis, spa baths and other necessities of modern high pressure existence.

In the early days, visitors came from near and far and were generally fulsome in their praises. The American Clara Kathleen Rogers wrote in her journal on December 7 1903 at the GFH opining that 'the view from her windows over the sea led her to believe that Ceylon must be heaven!' Another traveller wrote in 1911, 'In Colombo we got rickshaws and drove out to the Galle Face Hotel, a beautiful place with the surf thundering on the beach outside. In a cool and lofty dining hall we had an excellent and varied breakfast, and ate proper Eastern curry for the first time . . .'.

In the years following its construction the GFH became an important and fashionable centre of social life on the island. During the annual August Week festivities it was the focus of all the 'leading festivities and lavish entertainments which marked the gay period of Ceylon's capital' according to one contemporary account. The high point of the week was the lavish Race Ball. Previously, these had been held down the Green on the satinwood floor of the long hall on the upper storey of the Race Bungalow but, in 1883, the opening of the new Havelock Racecourse inland brought about its decline. The hotel was 'the' place to stay for travellers and for planters from up-country who filled the 200 bedrooms then in use. The hotel's porters met all steamers on arrival at the port, as well as the principal trains arriving at Fort Station. The hotel proudly boasted that "the management is entirely European" and, in the book *Twentieth Century Impressions of Ceylon* (published in London in 1907) there is an imposing picture of the German-born manager, Mr Conrad Peter in a splendid open carriage pulled by a fine looking black horse. He had arrived in Colombo in 1902 as assistant manager by way of London's Charing Cross Hotel and establishments in Scotland and New York.

On the corner of Galle Face Green Road and Kollupitiya Road, the hotel building would soon be agreeably set off by the Lutyens-like grand structure of Galle Face Court 2. The position of the hotel has always been unique and enviable facing as it did onto Galle Face Green, a natural asset without parallel, an almost green oasis in the centre of the capital. It had never been developed by successive colonial invaders: without fortification, it was simply regarded as too vulnerable to invasion by the next incursor, whoever that might be. In more modern times, the Taj Samudra has put down its roots almost next door to the GFH: a not unpleasant structure from the exterior and with all the hallmarks of luxury on the interior. But the Taj still lacks some of the style of the grand old lady of the Green.

In the 1920s, Francis Parkinson Keyes, associate editor of the American *Good Housekeeping* magazine came to Colombo by sea, relating the details of her stay in the GFH in her book *Coral Strands*, published in New York in 1926.

The trim little launch bore us swiftly ashore, and a moment later, having been passed through the Customs, we were speeding down along the coast drive, with the great, crested waves breaking noisily against it, on our way to our hotel; and soon found ourselves established in rooms such as we had not seen for many moons . . .

. . . the wind-swept rooms in Colombo, facing out to sea, furnished with every possible comfort and convenience, and each with a real bathroom, looked very inviting to us indeed; and the gentle-voiced, white robed 'boy' who instantly appeared on the scene saying: 'Lady want anything tonight? Lady ring if she wants me – I stay right here!' took us back to the lost treasures of China, who had ministered to us so magically . . .

The hotel remained largely untouched by two world wars. There was ballroom dancing to Teddy Wetherford and his Band. Carl Muller recalls that in the 1930s "guests would come to the sweeping verandas and lean over the wall to watch the people of Colombo 'take the air' on the Green." Often there would be music on the Green provided by the band of the Ceylon Light Infantry or the Police band and a large crowd would gather around the bandstand to applaud the stirring military music.

There was drama on Galle Face Green, right in front of the hotel, on Easter Sunday April 5 1942. The previous day, a Catalina flying boat had located the Japanese Imperial Fleet cruising at 30 knots towards Ceylon some 400 miles to the south west. After the Japanese attack on Pearl Harbour in December 1941, the fall of Singapore on February 15 1942 and the capture of the Indian Ocean islands of Nicobar and Andaman on March 26, it had seemed likely that Ceylon would be the next target. It was clear the attack was now on. At 5.25 a.m. the next morning, 223 aircraft took off from the Japanese carriers, now just 210 miles away. There were 125 Zero fighters escorting 97 Kate attack bombers. Thanks to the previous day's sighting and a vital radio message from the Catalina before it was downed, Ceylon had fighters ready to scramble from both Ratmalana and the aerodrome at the racecourse, and the Ceylon Garrison Artillery regiment was on high alert.

The principal target was Colombo Harbour. On Galle Face Green there was an anti-aircraft battery under the command of Major Mervyn Joseph. It was to be a busy day. During the engagement, the Japanese commander pulled back the fighter escorts believing his fleet might come under attack from aircraft of the British Eastern Fleet and the Galle Face battery claimed many 'kills'.

A Hurricane fighter piloted by a Flight Lieutenant McDonald was hit by Zeros and made a forced landing on Galle Face Green in front of the hotel. McDonald, who was unhurt, clambered out of the aircraft and demonstrated considerable *sang froid* immediately crossing Galle Road and entering the Colombo Club where he downed a double Scotch. It is recorded he then walked all the way back to Ratmalana, on the southern edge of the capital.

A few days later, men of the Royal Air Force rescue squadron dragged a shot down Zero fighter from their base at Kollupitiya, just down the road, and parked it on the Green right in front of the hotel. For several weeks, it was a treasure trove for souvenir hunters until it was so stripped down it became an eyesore and the city had the RAF remove the debris.

During the Second World War, Admiral Lord Louis Mountbatten, Supreme Commander South East Asia, whose headquarters were located at the Peradeniya Botanical Gardens in Kandy, was a regular visitor to the hotel. Then there was an obscure Greek prince who occasionally visited in the early days of the war. Prince Philip of Greece would become the husband of England's Queen Elizabeth but, in 1940, he was an impecunious 19 year-old midshipman serving in the British Royal Navy. One day in Colombo he spotted a green, two-door 1935 Standard 9, registration number X8468, which he bought for the then princely sum of 450 rupees: seven weeks navy pay. It was far from perfect. A cod liver oil bottle top served as a petrol cap but it was what the young prince most desired at that moment in time. He bought the car on the never-never, eventually paying it off. By a curious twist of fate, the car was acquired and restored in the 1950s by the soon to become GFH's Chairman, Cyril Gardiner, then the boss of Colombo's Autodrome. He restored it completely. When Prince Philip visited Ceylon in 1956, Cyril was delighted to show him the car again: it awaited him at the airport and, during the 1960s, it occupied pride of place at the end of the hotel lobby.

Standards were still rigorously maintained through those war years. In the early 1940s, the writer Christopher Ondaatje, then a young boy, recalls visiting the Royal Dining Room at the hotel, "probably Ceylon's most exclusive dining room at the time", with his father and mother. For his father, an up-country planter, the GFH was "my father's home away from home in Colombo". Ondaatje recalls it was a hot night and that the fans were not working. His father removed his jacket and draped it over the back of his chair. The waiter attending the table politely asked him to put it back on but his father refused. A second waiter approached with the same request. Again his father refused. Eventually, the headwaiter came over and advised, "I'm sorry, sir, but if you don't put on your jacket, you will have to leave."

Of course, these days the waiters will serve anybody in a 'Kiss Me Quick T-Shirt' or a pair of sawn-off denims . . .

During the 1950s and '60s the GFH was still the place to stay for the serious visitor to Colombo. The so-called five star hotels which now dot the city's landscape were not, as yet, even conceived. The GFH had only one competitor in the form of the Grand Oriental Hotel and its status was virtually unchallenged. It was also a fashionable night-time hangout for sophisticated local residents who patronised the Coconut Grove night club, entered from Galle Road, and where, in the octagonal supper room, they could dance the night away to Mignon Ratnam (later Fernando, after she married her manager) and The Jetliners.

***

Today the GFH remains a real seaside hotel: the waves break onto the beach just a few yards from your window overlooking the Indian Ocean, beyond the neatly manicured lawns and the chequerboard dance floor. To my mind, the best thing about the Galle Face is sitting on the terrace, if you are not availed of your own personal balcony, of an evening around 6 p.m. with a cold beer or a G&T watching the fiery red tropical sun setting slowly into the Indian Ocean beyond the gently stirring coconut palms. British Prime Minister Edward Heath stayed during the 1960s and wrote, "I was delighted to be able to sit on the balcony and watching the moonlight and listening to the waves while we discussed the problems of the international situation."

When I first visited in 1996, I reflected that it must be difficult to find a hotel surviving anywhere in the world so redolent of the charms of yesteryear. More of a palace than a hotel, aged retainers in pristine white military style uniforms, replete with red epaulettes and gold braid, cheerily saluted your progress through the magnificent, airy halls and over the creaking Burmese teak hardwood floors and fraying red carpets. Many of them then had worked in the hotel for more than half a century. The ratio of staff to guests was then a generous four to one. No employee had ever been sacked, apparently. But, on your way to your room, you did note the first signs of a certain eccentricity but - at first - you were maybe just mildly amused. Notices on the stairs like 'Silence is Golden' seemed a trifle quaint. 'Galle Face Hotel admires your decision not smoke', was courteous enough. A notice advising a room discount of $10 a night if you refrained from smoking seemed rather generous. 'Please do not smoke in bed because the ashes we find might be yours' was a little more threatening, and the one beside the lift, ' 'Please walk down. It's good for your health,' struck me as distinctly impertinent.

Your bedroom, if you are lucky, will be furnished with genuine, highly polished antiques, will likely be the size of half a dozen modern chain hotel rooms put together: the average size seems of the deluxe rooms to be around 30 foot by 20 foot. And all this could then be had for less than sixty or seventy dollars a night ... The King Emperor Suite, which has oft housed members of the British Royal family, is said to have the largest sitting room in any hotel anywhere in the world: it can comfortably accommodate 100 people for cocktails.

After watching the setting of the sun, you could then happily absorb the rest of the evening reading and chuckling over the stone plaques and wooden notice boards which are seemingly scattered at random through the extensive and grand public rooms. A letter of commendation from the Aga Khan is quoted, 'Happiness is the Galle Face Hotel'. Several marble and wooden plaques record the great, the good, the talented and the beautiful who have stayed. From the Duke of Edinburgh and Lord Louis Mountbatten to Emperor Hirohito of Japan and Pandit Nehru; the literary and artistic world is featured through the *aeges* of Noel Coward, Laurence Olivier, Cole Porter and George Bernard Shaw. Indeed, Coward made one of the first performances of *Mad Dogs and Englishmen* at a piano in the hotel, the song inspired by Ceylon. Travelling thespians are more than adequately represented by Trevor Howard, Bo Derek, Vivien Leigh and Ursula Andress.

In 1956, the hotel was transformed into the production office for what was to become the all time classic film, *Bridge over the River Kwai* starring, amongst others, Alec Guinness, David Lean and William Holden. Guinness enjoyed his days relaxing in the hotel after filming up country in Kandy, Kitulgale and Mahara, although Lean moved out to the Mount Lavinia Hotel for more peace and quiet away from the hubbub of film production. For ten months the hotel was awash with stars and film people. Chandran Rutnam, who worked on the production, remembers, "At 4.30 in the morning the buses would line up outside the hotel and the extras would troop on board to be taken upcountry for the day's filming."

The Australian High Commission opened its first office in Colombo in the hotel. Several BBC correspondents have worked from the hotel. The Foreign Correspondents' Association was founded in the hotel and still meets there regularly.

The charismatic owner Major (retired) Cyril Gardiner one day encountered actress Carrie Fisher strolling through the palatial entrance hall. Asked where she was staying, she replied, "Across the road at The Taj, but I don't like it . . . I'd rather be here, I think, but I've already paid for tonight" Rather like the Duke of Wellington, Cyril was never one to miss an opportunity. Cyril said he would send his boys over to move her things immediately and the first night would be on him. Amazingly, he didn't actually have a clue who Carrie Fisher was and was quite oblivious to her international cinematic fame. The next morning, the Chinese Embassy had a press conference at the hotel about some vital political or economic development. When Cyril mentioned who was staying at the hotel the journalists promptly abandoned the press conference and besieged the famous guest in her room.

Then there are those guests listed who are not so well known but who have had the grace to be complimentary about the hotel. Generally, that means journalists. Simon Winchester, the London *Sunday Times* journalist gets an honorable mention on the wall plaques (in return for his many honorable mentions of the hotel), as does the BBC's Mark Tully, himself a legend in South Asia where he is so synonymous with his role as a BBC reporter that many people think that 'Mark Tully' actually means 'journalist'. The BBC's John Rettie, who lived in the hotel for some two years when he was BBC correspondent in Colombo, also gets a mention drawing attention to his arrival at the hotel at three months of age: his father was an up-country tea planter. Another BBC man who did not get a mention is Chris Nuttall. He left because he said his telephone was tapped by government spies and departed for a hotel with a larger number of extensions.

Not mentioned is a more recent arrival, *The Sunday Times* journalist Marie Colvin whose trip to Sri Lanka would attract considerable notoriety. She came in 2001 to do a story on the Tamil Tigers. She was, it has to be said, inexperienced in the matter of Sri Lanka. It was her first visit to the island but she was determined to get behind the lines, and she set up her dramatic trip whilst staying at the GFH. The expedition would almost cost her her life and, indeed, did cost her an eye.

Forty-five year old Marie Colvin, an American citizen working for the London *Sunday Times*, is possibly one of the most respected war correspondents of her generation. She has exited spectacularly over the mountains from Chechnya and survived both war and the elements. In Sri Lanka, having crossed over without permission into LTTE territory, she attempted to re-cross at night across heavily defended frontlines. As she did so, and somehow her LTTE 'bodyguard' melted away into the black of the night, she came under Sri Lankan army mortar fire. Her body was pierced by four pieces of shrapnel: she received wounds to her eye, shoulder and thigh and sustained a bruised lung.

She wasn't a novitiate in international terms. The testimonials bear ample witness to her achievements. In year 2000, she was voted Foreign Reporter of the Year in the British Press Awards. The judges opined at the time, "The story of her escape from Chechnya was one of the great adventure stories of all time. They should make it into a film . . .". Also, the International Women's Media Foundation gave her the Courage in Journalism Award and noted "she has covered some of the worst bloodbaths of the last decade . . . *The Sunday Times* [found] Colvin needs a long rope". Colvin had covered Chechnya, Iraq, Kosovo and East Timor. She was one of the few journalists to remain in the UN compound in East Timor after the rest of the press pack was evacuated and she wrote critically of her male colleagues who had hopped on UN flights out of the war zone.

Sunday Times Foreign Editor Sean Ryan endorsed her decision to stay in the UN compound in East Timor, "She believed a media presence in the compound would provide the refugees with a measure of protection." So she stayed and she was – in print – enormously scathing of the male journalists who took off for safety in Australia. Probably, she stayed for the story rather than to preserve the lives of the locals. But she had guts in that situation all the same.

The *Sunday Times* trumpeted that she was the first journalist to work behind the lines of the rebel Tamil Tigers since 1995. A sub-editor's little mistake, I assume. I had been 13 times to Sri Lanka in the six years before her visit. She was by no means the first journalist to cross the lines in the previous seven years. The thing was that those of us who had done it had carried out the operation safely and discreetly. Indeed, a trip to Sri Lanka was hardly complete without a cup of Ceylon tea with the Tigers. . .

She was clearly impressed with the Tigers, judging from her article which appeared in *The Sunday Times*. It advises, "The LTTE emerged in 1983, when Sinhalese mobs turned on the Tamils, slaughtering hundreds with machetes". I am afraid her explanation of the genesis of the conflict was quite at variance with the historical record: the slaughter she refers to did take place but it was a reaction to a massacre by the LTTE leader Velupillai Prabakharan of an army unit in northern Sri Lanka. I didn't blame Marie Colvin for getting that wrong; I just guessed she didn't know the long-running Sri Lanka story so well. She was what is known in the media business as a 'parachutist': a media star dropped into a story she neither knew intimately nor understood particularly well.

However, she should at least have realised that during her peregrination behind the lines her press visa had expired. She arrived in the capital Colombo on March 27 and obtained 14 days press accreditation from the Ministry of Information. Strangely, she missed her appointment with Foreign Minister Lakshman Kadirgamar and dropped out of sight until April 16 when she approached the forward defence lines of the Sri Lanka army together with a unit of the rebel Tamil Tigers. Their approach was, predictably, picked up by an army listening post, using sophisticated equipment supplied by the Israelis. They came under fire; Colvin was injured and she was abandoned by her LTTE guides.

To flout the visa requirements in a Third World country is foolish bravado. OK you can often buy your way out of trouble but it is a cavalier way to behave. The fact that she was abandoned by her 'hosts' as soon as they came under fire would suggest to those experienced in the ways of the war in Sri Lanka that she had actually been 'set up': her death at the hands of government troops would have attracted seriously bad publicity to the Sri Lankan government.

Her *modus operandi* was at best naïve and, at worst, stupid. To approach a military forward defence line in the company of a group of rebels is not brave but foolhardy.

But the worst thing about Colvin's little adventure on the sunshine island was that she poisoned the well for those of us who had worked painstakingly on this story for many years. Since her being injured, the Sri Lanka government posted on its website a notice: "The facts that have emerged so far indicate that she has had her own secret agenda with the LTTE . . . In view of the seriousness of this event the Ministry of Defence has conveyed its concern to the Ministry of Foreign Affairs and informed the Sri Lankan Missions abroad to be cautious when recommending journalists for visas." Indeed, right up until the middle of February 2002 it was virtually impossible for foreign journalists to get behind the lines – although local journos were permitted – thanks to the Colvin Factor. The Ministry of Defence's Mr Austin Fernando refused me permission in January of that year, despite an apparent outbreak of peace. I went anyway. But I didn't sneak over and back by night . . .

Her tale of derring-do in Sri Lanka raised, however, important issues. At one level, there was the fact that many foreign correspondents – fashionably referred to as war correspondents – regularly risk life and limb to bring the truth about what is happening in far flung and inhospitable places to our breakfast tables. Of course, we applaud this. But things are not always as they appear. . . that derring-do can be singularly misplaced.

I wrote at the time in a British newspaper, 'Journalists will now find it much harder to get visas and cover this story. Get well soon, Marie. But do us a favour and please don't go back to Sri Lanka.'

***

There are some mystery men on those plaques in the Galle Face Hotel whose fame or fortune has somehow been eclipsed by the passage of time. There is one Tigger Stack Ramsay-Brown M C (who he?). There were the days when the 'money' stayed at the hotel: the likes of the Aga Khan, John D Rockefeller, Alfred Krupp and the Queen's jeweller Eric Asprey. The hotel's four Royal suites commemorate the visits of royalty from England, Thailand, Denmark and Holland.

The carefully carved marble plaques are reminiscent of the days when anybody who was anybody would stay at the GFH when in Ceylon. The extravagantly moustachioed K C Kuttan - 'Chattu' as he is known - worked at the Galle Face Hotel for more than sixty years. Born in Kerala, India, he left his home and took the ferry to Talaimannar and from there came to Colombo in 1938, working initially in the tea-rubber houses on Slave Island. He joined the staff at the hotel in 1942 shortly after the Japanese bombing raid on Colombo. Then full board cost only Rs. 45 and his salary was Rs 20 a month. Chattu started as a waiter. It took him fifty years to gravitate to the front door!

Kuttan became almost as much of a landmark in Colombo as the hotel itself. He must be the most photographed person in the city, always a firm favourite with guests and travelers greeting them, as he does, with palms together in traditional Ceylonese style. His distinctive moustache, white brass buttoned coat, sarong and bronzed visage have graced the pages of newspapers and magazines internationally and, despite his years, he told me he could stand for over eight hours without resting. Until comparatively recently, he walked three miles every day to the hotel to work. "Now I walk one mile," he says. "It keeps me healthy." One newspaper described him as straight from the pages of P G Wodehouse.

19

At a ceremony to mark 60 years at the GFH, the Chairman of the Ceylon Tourist Board, Renton de Alwis, observed, "Kuttan, you are in the forefront of the hotel industry." A happy, if rather poor, pun.

He met all the famous guests who came to stay and in 2002 was still in regular touch with Arthur C Clarke. Chattu says fondly, "There was a time when all the high people who visited came here to stay. This was place was Number One. Now there are many hotels . . .". His voice trails off disappointedly. In fact, until the early 1970s, the GFH was the only hotel of any real substance in central Colombo. Then, the first of the modern five star hotels opened. First to be built was the Hotel Ceylon Intercontinental (now the Ceylon Continental), facing the GFH at the other end of the Green, and in which Cyril Gardiner became a director and Deputy Chairman in 1970. The GFH actually invested in it but no longer has any interest. It was severely damaged in the 1996 Central Bank bomb blast and subsequently ceased to be part of the Intercontinental chain.

The late seventies and early eighties have been described as the 'Golden Years' for Sri Lanka generally, and Colombo particularly. It was a time of peace and relative plenty and economic reforms started to open up the country to business. There were tourists a-plenty and hotel building started all over the island as existing hotels found themselves consistently overbooked. This seems remarkable today after years of war have driven away the tourists and Colombo's deluxe five star hotels find themselves often with occupancy rates of less than 30%. The Ceylon Continental was joined by the Galadari Meridien, just a hundred yards away, which was due to open in 1983 but deferred opening until October 1984, as war broke out in the north and bloody riots swept the south. The Galadari later became a Marriott Hotel but, like the Ceylon Intercontinental, ultimately left the chain in difficult trading conditions. Meantime, the Lanka Oberoi, just a few hundred yards from the GFH down Galle Road, had opened. Despite the violence, hoteliers who had put plans in hand for building during rather better times proceeded optimistically, with a Hilton Hotel rising after 1983 to open in '87, next to the Galadari, and a Taj Hotel – the Samudra – built right next to the racecourse building on Galle Green. Apart from the Trans Asia Hotel, built a few years later and located a further kilometer inland, all of Colombo's five star hotels – and the GFH which made no such vulgar claim – were clustered within a single one and a half kilometer-long block.

***

These days the Lion Flag of Sri Lanka flies in front of the hotel before the portico. On Independence Day there are several of them but other national days are solemnly celebrated with the flags of foreign states. Independence came to Ceylon on February 4 1948. In those heady days, the Lion Flag was the symbol of unity, friendship and harmony, without a hint of the traumas which would split the state asunder. The flag's colour and imagery encompassed all peoples on the island: Sinhala, Tamil and the Yonaka, or Muslim population. The 2,000 year-old Lion Flag of the Sinhlaese King Dutugemunu is often considered the oldest flag in the world: the lion holding a sword upright in its right forepaw stands for justice and righteousness; the four boa leaves symbolize compassion, kindness, prosperity and equanimity. In 1948, the flag was modified to include the two vertical strips – of saffron and green – in recognition of the two minority communities of Sri Lanka.

A bust of Arthur C Clarke has sprouted in the Grand Entrance Hall of the GFH in recent years. Clarke has finished several of his books in seclusion in the Chairman's Suite, one of the largest in the hotel, most lately *3001: The Final Oddyssey*. Clarke loves to stay in the hotel for its peace and quietude, despite the fact that he owns a luxury home not far away in one of Colombo's most select residential districts. As the

Facade

hotel is such a favourite of Clarke, several films made from his books, like *Fountains of Paradise*, have been partially shot within its precincts.

The Afterword of *3001* pays generous tribute to CG. 'Finally, and most important of all: my deepest thanks to my old friend Cyril Gardiner, Chairman of the Galle Face Hotel, for the hospitality of his magnificent (and enormous) personal suite while I was writing this book. He gave me a Tranquility Base in a time of troubles. I hasten to add that, even though it may not provide such extensive imaginary landscapes, the facilities of the Galle Face are far superior to those offered by the 'Gannymede' and never in my life have I worked in more comfortable surroundings... It seems appropriate that a project begun in one famous hotel – New York's Chelsea, that hotbed of genuine and imitation genius – should be concluded in another, half a world away. But it's strange to hear the monsoon-lashed Indian Ocean roaring just a few yards outside my window, instead of the traffic along far-off and fondly remembered 23rd Street.' As Clarke made the final corrections to the manuscript, he learned that his friend Cyril had died and observed, "It is some comfort to know that he had already seen the above acknowledgement and had been delighted with it."

Film makers often come to the hotel to shoot their movies. One Italian director told me, "Everything is here, untouched. We save all the money on the set budget." A film chronicling the fall of President Marcos in The Philippines – the HBO production *A Dangerous Life* - was shot in Colombo after the government there declined to host the film makers. The Chairman's paneled office became Marcos's bedroom and the vast, high white-painted Victorian-era ballroom, with its arched and balustraded balconies and whirling ceiling fans, needed virtually no work to transform into the dictator's extravagant Malakan Palace. Cyril Gardiner was exceptionally keen to have the film makers at the hotel and said that they could use it as a location free of charge if they took fifteen rooms. The film company did indeed take 15 rooms but they lay empty: everybody stayed at the modern Lanka Oberoi, which was rather more to their taste. When Cyril found out he was not pleased and demanded that the rooms be used. The company relented and sent the film carpenters to stay at the GFH. This made the Chairman even less pleased. He complained to the producers, "I ask you to send me some actors and you send me your carpenters."

In a local film on the rebellion against the British in the 1840s, a room in what was then the Queen's House (now the President's House), was recreated in a first floor bedroom. The filming went fine but when it was screened sharper minds espied a fatal anachronism: the portrait hung on the wall was of what was then a very young Queen Victoria was, in fact, of a very elderly Queen!

Roshan Seth stayed at the GFH whilst filming *Iqbal*. Noel Coward's *Ebb Tide* was shot in Sri Lanka and the shoot brought not only Coward to the hotel but also the star Ali Khan who would later write of how he danced in the ballroom to the popular song of the day, *Unforgettable*. Stephen Spielberg was a regular visitor when he was in Sri Lanka to shoot *Indiana Jones and The Temple of Doom*, although he stayed at the Lanka Oberoi. Chandran Rutnam, who organized his booking at the Oberoi, came to regret it. He went along to the Oberoi to meet the newly arrived Spielberg who was booked into the best suite which had been decorated with flowers and supplied with expensive goodies. He was appalled by what he found. "When I went into the suite I found that the management had made a mistake and put some other guest called Seberg into the room. There he was sitting amidst Spielberg's flowers and eating his chocolates." Clearly, he should have booked him into the GFH.

Some scenes from *Elephant Walk* were shot in the hotel and the stars, including Peter Finch and Vivian Leigh, stayed at the GFH. For Vivian Leigh, it was an unhappy stay. She suffered a nervous breakdown, complaining that a devil had got hold of her. Laurence Olivier came out from London and took her home. Chandran Rutnam remembers, "She left the hotel on a stretcher." Leigh was replaced by Elizabeth Taylor and scenes already shot had to be cut or edited to replace the original star, who was never ever to fully recover.

The hotel was even persuaded to invest 500,000 rupees in one film shot on the premises. Even though it was to star Ben Kingsley (he walked out after a week), the film, *God King* directed by Lester James Pieris and produced by Dimitri de Grunwald, never saw the light of day.

There are rather fonder memories of the movie business. To this day, staff at the hotel remember actress Ursula Andress dancing in the ballroom on New Year's Night in 1976 to the music of Tony Felice and his Blue Star Band. She stayed at the hotel whilst filming *Mountain in the Jungle* with James Keitch.

The hotel has featured in several books. In Jeanne Cambrai's thriller, *Murder in the Pettah*, published in 2001, the hotel is accurately summed up. 'The Galle Face Hotel is a relic of the past that has not lent itself to modernization. It is a reminder, however, that the British once ruled the island with a Victorian taste for large over small, comfort over style, and good manners no matter what.' In Christopher Ondaatje's *The Man-Eater of Punanai* 'The Galle Face Hotel still symbolizes the colonial era in Ceylon. It's a magnificent palace by the ocean, with palm trees in the lobby, waiters wearing elaborate uniforms, fans whirring on the ceilings, and an aura of genteel society.' In Carl Muller's novel *Colombo*, the Galle Face Hotel, seen from the Green by two young lovers, is 'a chocolate gateaux of amber lights and frosted fluorescence ... Galle Face Hotel is one of the few memorable buildings in Colombo today. And it is known so well and remembered so fondly by many people the world over.'

Peter Adamson's *Facing Out to Sea*, published in 1997, is a novel actually set in the hotel. Although, curiously, it is not specifically named, it is unmistakable. 'To the south, facing out onto the end of the Green, stood the oldest and most dignified of the capital's hotels, its low white façade arched and pillared . . .' Adamson's book, something of a literary *tour de force*, is descriptively powerful, especially in its scenes drawn from the poverty and slums of Colombo, and strained labour relations at the hotel, but suffers from a highly unlikely story line: a relationship between an English female, a high powered company director at one of those turning points in life beloved of novelists, and a waiter at the hotel, which putative relationship brings inevitable disaster. The unlikely relationship brings, in the view of other staff, 'disorder because she had not kept her place, not maintained her part in the framework which allowed others also to have their place.' Adamson does pick up on some of the hotel's more delightful *minutiae*, like the Chairman's breakfast, which becomes Miles Perera's 'little light luncheon' in his private dining room for 'the more presentable of the hotel's guests . . . It was the equivalent of an invitation to dine at the captain's table'. Indeed, in the long tradition of the GFH's generosity towards writers, Adamson and his wife were given free board and lodging for two months while he researched the book. "Cyril was always generous like that with writers," says former general manager Lalith Rodrigo. He was also conscious of the mythic power of the printed word and the perpetuation of the GFH international legend. However, he was a trifle miffed that the hotel never even received a copy of the book.

Again, the hotel is not specifically named in Martin Wickramasinghe's well known Sinhala novel *Gamperaliya*, but it is fairly evident that it is the place where the rural hero, Piyal, comes to work in the capital, after his rejection in love by the aristocratic Kaisaruwattes. Deemed unfit to marry their daughter, he first works in the Galle Face Hotel and later acquires the contract to supply eggs and fruit there. This is the foundation of his success as a bourgeois trader in the city and he later returns and gets his girl. The book was made into a renowned classic film by Lester James Pieris.

However, it is Arthur C Clarke who remains the *eminence grise* of the hotel's literary associations. Near the bust of Clarke, in the lofty reception hall, stands a stone water trough topped with frangipani petals. Birds nesting in the rafters above can swoop down to drink.

> *Flowers for you*
> *Water for the Birds*
> *That flit and twitter*
> *Musically up and down*

The words are engraved on a pillar. The hotel boasts the only breeding colony of house sparrows in Colombo. They have been there since the colonial days of the hotel, which refers to them as its 'special guests', and they nest without interruption on the tops of the tall pillars of the Grand Entrance. Cyril – a good Buddhist - was notably protective of all the forms of wildlife which inhabited his hotel. He put a stop to the efforts of some of his staff when they attempted to clear away the sparrows' nest; refused to do anything about the dozens of crows which perch eagle-eyed, so to speak, around the terrace and then swooped down to carry off the sandwich of some unwitting tourist; and even was frequently reluctant to do anything about the cockroaches.

***

The plaques and notices are enduring memorials to the hotel's eccentric owner, deceased in 1997, Cyril Gardiner, always referred to by his staff as The Chairman in the sort of reverent tones the Chinese once reserved for Mao Tse Tung. Larger than life, often charming, frequently uncompromising, if not totally intransigent, Gardiner was a true autocrat within his own four walls.

He joined the board of the hotel in 1960, bought what was then a small stake and became Chairman six years later, although his grandfather had served on the original board of directors. Within the decade he and his companies would own 90%. The method by which this was achieved was not without controversy: in September 1966, the restructuring of the hotel company was challenged in court by one of the shareholders, The Ceylon Insurance Company Ltd. This would be but the first of many legal actions over the years precipitated by efforts to refinance or restructure the Galle Face Hotel Company. In the litigation launched in 1966 it was alleged in the court submissions that 'alterations in the articles of association of the company are circulated to entrench Mr Cyril Gardiner and his nominees or henchmen (*sic.*) in the control and management of the Galle Face Hotel Co. Ltd.'. CG would dig himself out of this action, as he would do with others over the years.

Cyril Gardiner's personal interest in the GFH grew directly out of his business in the motor trade. He was managing director of Tuckers, the General Motors franchise holders in Ceylon, and also Founder President of The Autodrome Ltd, a business he created to handle Opel cars and Bridgestone Tyres. Tuckers Autodrome staged an annual Autorama at the GFH to introduce new models, which were duly photographed in front of the hotel together with a bevy of beautiful girls. He, and the companies he controlled, together owned around 90% of the equity in the hotel. Given its size and position, the hotel represents one of the most substantial, undeveloped pieces of real estate left in Colombo. But its owners have steadfastly refused to exploit that asset. Indeed, Cyril Gardiner – wisely – paid off the hotel's mortgage and completely closed the south wing to reduce running costs on the vast establishment which used to be termed the 'resort within the city'.

In his schooldays at St Joseph's, he won prizes for both elocution and singing and, having marched proudly down the aisle so be-medalled, he became known as 'Goering'.

I once had cause to call Gardiner the Basil Fawlty of South Asia. Basily Fawlty was, of course, that wonderful comic creation of British comedian John Cleese: a manic character presiding erratically over a seaside guest house in the British resort of Torquay. In the spring of 1996, the Galle Face was going through, let's say, a difficult patch. In the course of a week's stay, you couldn't help but notice that the aged roof was leaking copiously on the stairs. The staff of a lunchtime grabbed placards and demonstrated at the main entrance over Gardiner's conservative view of staff remuneration, before promptly returning to work in the afternoon. The terrace dining area resembled a shower cubicle in heavy rain and as I tucked into my damp curry and rice I could not help but observe a trio of half drowned rats emerge from a drain cover. The water ran brown from the taps. The electricity regularly failed several times a day as the aged generators attempted to cope with the vagaries of the Sri Lankan national grid. Maintaining an adequate supply of electricity is an apparently insoluble, island-wide problem. Undue reliance on rain to feed a hydro-based system has meant years of power cuts The Ceylon Electricity Board seems to have tried everything: in January 2001 it reluctantly admitted to the engagement of a Buddhist monk to visit the reservoir areas and chant *manthras* for rain. This had no immediate effect on a parlous situation probably attributable to global climate change.

Back in 1996 things were bad. Although the lights were successfully powered by the hotel generators, they could not cope with the air conditioning. Things got pretty warm. And, in the heat of the night, the insects came out to play.

About 1.30 one morning my *sang froid* snapped as the flying cockroaches, having knocked themselves out by flying into the walls at high speed, tumbled around me on the bed. As a phalanx of room boys attacked the incursors with their shoes, beating them to death on the carpet, I summoned Cyril to the telephone.

He appeared to listen patiently to my complaint. Nobody had warned me, however, that he was particularly protective of his cockroach population. "Mr Harris, you must understand," he began with an ominously wearisome tone to his voice, "that these cockroaches have been here since before man was on this planet. They tell me that they will be here even after a nuclear war. What can you really expect me to do about them? If you don't like my cockroaches then I suggest you move to the Hilton Hotel."

I did. This was hardly the anticipated sympathetic response of the remorseful hotelier. At least, when I checked out, the cashier told me, "Mr Gardiner says there is no bill for you, Mr Harris ..." The hotel provided a car which swept me up to the Hilton, past the ranks of protesting hotel staff. They weren't protesting at my leaving, of course, but rather at the fact that their share of the 10% service charge wasn't filtering through into their wage packets. 'We are not againis (*sic.*) tourists. Our demands are reasonable' read one placard. Although there was quite a lot of shouting, it was all fairly low key on the world scale of industrial protests.

Cyril's love for the wildlife populating his hotel was sometimes difficult to understand. The sparrows and the chipmunks are harmless enough, to be sure. The crows, the cockroaches and the rats were quite another thing. When the writer and Canadian philanthropist Christopher Ondaatje stayed in the early 1990s he carefully placed his solid gold Rolex watch on the bedside table. When he awoke in the morning he was appalled to find it gone. As he climbed into his dressing gown to berate the management, he espied the watch being pulled through a hole in the wall by a large brown rat. In the nick of time, he pulled the Rolex from the jaws of the rodent. The leather strap was quite ruined, much of it having been gnawed away, but at least the glittering watch was saved.

During the 1950s a similar sort of incident occurred although without such an immediate denouement. Dozing on her balcony, a well heeled lady guest took off her cherished and very large diamond ring. When she awoke, the ring was gone. The then chairman of the Hotel, Sir John Tarbert, had the hotel turned upside down in the search for the ring. All of the staff was comprehensively grilled but of the ring there was no trace. Such was the enforced and persistent interrogation that there was much discontent below stairs. Almost ten years later, one of the coconut trees on the seafront was felled. A crow's nest tumbled from the tree and there is the framework of the nest there glittered the lost diamond ring . . .

Many years earlier there had been industrial action after Cyril engaged the services of an old army friend, the recently retired Brigadier Jayaweera. The Brigadier duly set himself on a campaign of sweeping changes and installation of army-style discipline. A strike developed and senior management, including the Brigadier, set about keeping the place running. This, in turn, resulted in a spirited demo outside the hotel. A friend of mine, a retired general, received a panic-stricken call at army headquarters, just across the road. The call seemed to suggest that some sort of terrible insurrection was taking place. Together with some other senior officers he made his way to the hotel.

The sight of the placards occasioned the army chaps some mirth. "One read 'Yesterday a brigadier, today a dishwasher' and when I saw that I knew these fellows had a sense of humour and couldn't be any real threat," recalls the general, "We made our way to the terrace, had some beers and a good laugh." Served by senior management, of course.

After the infestation problem, the next several trips I stayed in the Hilton. There were no cockroaches. Everything worked absolutely perfectly, the staff were equally delightful and virtually your every wish was satisfied. But it was the archetypal international hotel experience: essentially charmless and very boring. And then the Tamil Tiger terrorists blew up the area, anyway, in a bid to destroy the adjacent twin World Trade Towers. All long before September 11 2001.

So, I found myself in January 1997 back at the Galle Face

with all its elegant fading grandeur. Although I tried my very best to resist the feeling, I really felt I was coming home. There were still, as British travel writer Simon Winchester once put it, the 'waiters who seem to have been standing on the same spot, beside the same potted palms, for half a century'. The telephones were still unpredictable. The fax went down for two or three days at a time.

One evening, a uniformed servant smilingly presented me with a telephone message written in beautiful script. I duly tipped him 20 rupees and he padded off happily. Only then I discerned the message bringing news of a six figure offer for some property in Scotland was three days old. When I telephoned my solicitor, it had expired. But, somehow, it did not seem to matter underneath the palms at the GFH . . .

Breakfast on the terrace was still a leisurely affair. The bill could take twenty minutes to materialize and the legendary coffee was still as undrinkable; and the tea had the taste and consistency of tar. There was no bar to stand at in those days. Cyril was a strict teetotaler. However, drinks were served to table by waiters in starched sarongs. Cyril once admitted, "This hotel is not perfect but I think it is delightfully imperfect." You could just imagine the irascible John Cleese, in the persona of Basil Fawlty, saying that.

Around the time of the mooted deal with Raffles he insisted that even under the proposed new regime there would not be a cocktail bar in the refurbished hotel. "People who want to watch the sunset over a couple of gin and tonics are most welcome. But I don't want the heavy boozers you get in a bar." Indeed, he boasted that he never hosted a single cocktail party in his life. His wife, Mavis, hosted a lunch at the hotel where there was no alcohol, no tobacco and no food 'prohibited by any of the great religions'. He admitted to serving drinks at just one dinner he hosted, on the grounds that "otherwise no one would have come!" but he did famously observe back in 1980 that "hoteliers need not sell liquor to make spectacular profits". Appropriately enough, he was addressing the inaugural meeting of the National Association on Alcohol and Drug Dependence at the GFH. "We have been told that the end does not justify the means. I am now going to prove to you that when the means are honorable, they do not need justification and that the results are spectacular." He went on to say that he closed the hotels' bars in 1978. "During the following year, the hotel made a profit of Rs. 7.3 million. For the second year, there were no stand-up bars although liquor was of course served. . . . During the same period the GFH discouraged smoking with a 'No Smoking' lounge and displayed several signs . . .I practise what I preach." A little pompously, he recalled the motto of his old school, St Joseph's, *mens sana in corpore sano,* "Your prayer must be that you may have a sound mind in a sound body."

At somebody else's hotel – the Bentota Beach Hotel – he noted that the establishment's public relations person, a most attractive young woman, was chain smoking. When he checked out, he left behind a sealed envelope containing a leaflet warning on the dangers of smoking.

Gardiner gave a lunch in the hotel in 1984 for Queen Ingrid of Denmark, after whom he duly named a suite, and after the meal she noticed a No Smoking sign. Though reportedly 'craving' a cigarette, even She forbore to smoke in Gardiner's forbidding presence.

His preoccupation with healthy living did not come to his aid when he was involved in a serious motor accident at the roundabout at the corner by the hotel. In the 1960s he was in the habit of going for a daily drive with two old friends around Galle Face Green. His dear friend Dr Henry Perera died, and Dr Sivali Ratwatte was seriously hurt, when the Benz motor car they were traveling in was hit by a lorry. Cyril miraculously survived when he thrown out of the back seat and through the rear door.

In the 1970s there was a period when there was a short-lived enthusiasm for introducing international hospitality standards to the GFH. A management deal was struck with Regent Hotels, proprietors of some of the best hotels in Asia. The honeymoon period lasted just so long. One manager arrived back after the weekend to find Cyril had locked him out of his room and he was obliged to seek residency elsewhere. Eventually, Regent sued the GFH. A court order requiring the hotel to observe the conditions of the management contract served on October 11 1978 was duly ignored by the irascible Chairman. When the area manager of Regent Hotels tried to check in the next morning, Gardiner approached him at reception and tersely advised, "There is no room for you here."

Asked by the representative of Regent to hand over management of the hotel as per the contract, Gardiner allegedly said, "Never, never, never." He got up from his office chair and affirmed, "Do you think I will take a gun in my hands and commit suicide because you have gone to court? I will fight you all the way."

This altercation resulted in Gardiner being fined for contempt of court three weeks later. The judge observed, "The offence in this case is aggravated by the fact that the accused is not an illiterate person ..." Gardiner was given two months to pay a fine of Rs. 2,500. Regent returned to court ten days later to press the main substance of its case against Gardiner and at the beginning of December an interim injunction was issued against The Galle Face Hotels Company Ltd and Cyril Gardiner. The injunction restrained them from 'preventing or obstructing' Regent 'from exercising the right of absolute management and control".

Cyril ignored the court's instructions and, as a result, in March 1980, the Supreme Court convicted Gardiner and the other directors of the company of contempt of court. In addition to ordering that Gardiner and the others be committed to jail and incarcerated there until their contempt was purged, the Supreme Court fined Cyril Gardiner Rs.

25,000, in default of which he was to serve 12 months rigorous imprisonment. "The default sentences shall commence to run after the contempt is purged," ordered the Chief Justice.

The Directors were held to have purged their contempt after lodging funds with the court but Regent never got back into the building to run the hotel. "Eventually Regent got tired and simply went away," says former managing director Lalith Rodrigo.

In 1993 another international hotel group appeared on the scene. A joint venture agreement was signed by Cyril Gardiner at Raffles Hotel in Singapore on August 4 of that year. Under the agreement, the biggest real estate company in Singapore, DBS Land, took 25% of the joint venture project and the GFH retained 75%. Management of the hotel for a period of 30 years was to be in the hands of Raffles International, with CG retaining control of public relations, at which he was such an accomplished proponent, and secretarial services, the shopping village at the back of the hotel, and the travel counter. The hotel would undergo renovation and the number of rooms would be doubled (doubtless by making them smaller as well as by renovating the semi-derelict south wing). This was clearly about to become a serious Raffles Operation. You could not help but assume that The Raffles Hotel group really had their beady eyes on total control of the GFH. There were even rumours circulating of an imminent sale, but Cyril added in emphatic bold letters at the foot of a piece of advertising he issued, 'GFH will never be sold'. At one point, people said Cyril's widow, Mavis, didn't want to sell but rumour had it that his son, Sanjeev, would have liked to bring the 19th century kicking and screaming into the 21st . . . I felt distinctly ambivalent about this. It would be nice if things worked. But I was not so sure I wanted that three by four yard room at $500 a night.

Upon his return to the island, Cyril reassured the doubters. "Further upgrading . . . will be implemented with tender loving care and with a deep sense of ambience and history. The distinctive character of the GFH will be preserved at all costs." To a newspaper in Melbourne, Australia, he was equally reassuring, "Trust me, there'll be no shopping mall, no theme restaurants, no fake English pub." The deal collapsed, however, just as the Regent Hotels one had earlier. The collapse was unexpected. In April 1994, a cocktail party was hosted by the new operators to celebrate the new partnership. This was more than a little embarrassing for Cyril, staunchly opposed to serving the dreaded alcohol, and he remained outside the ballroom whilst most of the guests merrily toasted the future inside.

The rumour mill reported that the deal fell down on nomenclature; others said that Cyril was alarmed at the costs involved and the inevitable result on room prices: the initial investment was said to run to US$7 million in the first year, going up to $19 million within three. At the time, CG said, "I don't want it to exceed more than $19 million because then the hotel will become too expensive ..." And, the GFH would *not*, under any circumstances, be renamed the Raffles Galle Face Hotel ... One senses that when it came to the crunch, Cyril could not bear to be parted from his beloved GFH.

Relations with Raffles were not soured, however, by the breakdown. Shortly after CG's death, his widow, Mavis, received a fax from Richard Helfer, Chairman and CEO of Raffles International, "Cyril was a man of strong principles who participated fully and passionately in everything he did. Exuding great warmth and sincerity to all he met, he had grown to become a very good friend over the last seven years."

Ironically, it was reported early in 1994, as the Raffles deal collapsed, that the previous year had been the most profitable in the history of the hotel. Gardiner had trenchantly observed in 1991, "The thicker the carpet, the thinner the dividend . .. the GFH has existed for over 125 years with tiled and polished teak floors and without wall to wall carpeting.

"Why should one heat a room with wall to wall carpeting utilizing valuable foreign exchange and at the same time spend still more foreign exchange to cool the room adequately?"

In 1992-93, turnover had increased by 34% from SLR 46 million to SLR 62 million, and profit before tax was SLR 19.3 million: previous year had been SLR 9.7 million.. Declared the Chairman, "The GFH is one of the highest, if not the highest, income tax-paying hotel companies in Sri Lanka." Of course, the hotel was not carrying the incredible burden of debt which all the new hotels were saddled with after construction in the 1980s against the backdrop of war in the north and civil insurrection in the south, which played havoc with visitor numbers and turned the bottom line from black to red overnight.

No major renovations were carried out to the hotel after 1970. Maintenance and repairs, however, continued to be a drain on finances. As Chairman Gardiner put it, "The annual repairs and maintenance costs of the GFH buildings are understandably high as these buildings . . . are exposed to the elements, particularly the salty sea breeze blowing freely through its wide open doors and corridors." Son Sanjeev gradually renovated and improved the establishment without detracting from its decaying and distinctive charm but it was still delightfully imperfect as the 21st century dawned.

In 2002, your bill was still handwritten from enormous ledgers. Computerised accounting had yet to make its appearance at the GFH. Ten years earlier, travel writer Simon Winchester wrote in America's *Traveller* Magazine, 'The place is far too pleasingly primeval, in the view of its many admirers, ever to be modernized. It must not become an expensive and ersatz version of its early self, refurbished into parody.'

When radical change seemed to be just around the corner in the late 1990s, I always advised people to get themselves to the GFH for the experience whilst it survived as an anachronism. After her visit, Carrie Fisher wrote to Gardiner summing up the appeal of his establishment, "You could be alone here without ever feeling lonely." No computerised bill to make you feel just a number, some impersonal, meaningless transient.

Cyril passed on to the great hotel in the sky after a heart attack in September 1996. He was 74 years of age. The rumour almost immediately started that he had expired on the dance floor of the ballroom. Alas, that was not the case. He had been dancing at the nearby Trans Asia Hotel at his niece's wedding when he became unwell; sadly that prevented him from attending the wedding of his son Sanjeev the next day. It would somehow have been far more appropriate if he had become ill at his own beloved GFH. He often proclaimed the health benefit of ballroom dancing. He said there was no better way to exercise than on the dance floor with a beautiful woman in your arms. Despite his demise, his spirit stubbornly remains, filling the vast, echoing corridors of the GFH.

His son, Sanjeev, became the Chairman of the Hotel. When he is at the hotel, he works from a vast paneled office overlooking the Indian Ocean. Favored guests may be lucky enough to be invited to a Chairman's Breakfast; a small, select gathering where the conversation is far and away the best feature of the occasion. Then your name can join all those illustrious others in the Visitors' Book.

Colonial time machine

The first western travellers perceived what is today known as Sri Lanka, with its luscious landscapes, white beaches, smiling, graceful inhabitants and the bounteous fruit of the trees, as some sort of paradise on earth. Today Sri Lanka is, indeed, a place of beauty and charm: and startling paradoxes. Marco Polo thought it the 'the finest island of its size in the world'. This little piece of paradise was known to the British as Ceylon; to the Romans as Taprobane; to the Dutch as Ceylan; and to Muslim traders as Serendib, the island of serendipity, the word coined by Horace Walpole in the 18th century in his fairy tale *The Three Princes of Serendib*. The local minority Tamil population called it Eelam and the majority Sinhalese restored their own historical name Sri Lanka in 1972 in a fit of inappropriate socialist and Sinhala nationalist pique. Ceylon somehow seems immeasurably more graceful and resonant as a name.

This country is at once all things to all men and one mighty enigma: beautiful, baffling and seductive. A succession of colonial incursors – Portuguese, Dutch and British – invaded and stamped their mark on this small piece of paradise. That mark was not indelible. More than half a century of independence has seen an end not just to the name 'Ceylon', which is maintained by just a few organs of government like the Ceylon Tourist Board, but also to many of the old colonial artefacts and ways.

The last inhabitant of the Indian Ocean island of Sri Lanka to meet HRH The Prince of Wales, before he took off for Nepal on his South Asian tour in 1998, was a Sergeant Major in the Sri Lankan army. Truth to tell, they didn't have much to say to each other although the encounter was memorable for a Prince probably relieved to be leaving behind possibly his most dangerous assignment ever.

Before making his way up the steps to his aircraft he actually fed Sgt Maj Kandula, who has been four years in the army, bananas from a silver salver. This may sound like some anachronistic colonial charade straight from the movie set of *The Man Who Would Be King*, but needs must reveal that the bearer of this honorary rank in the army is a small Ceylonese elephant. Sgt Maj Kandula enjoys his rank on the grounds of the financial requirements for his feeding and maintenance.

His Colonel explained to me the curious status of the regimental mascot of the 1st Regiment of the Ceylon Light Infantry, "If we didn't give him this rank we would not be able to draw down the money to keep him . . .". This, of course, is a neat way to sidestep the former colony's multi-layered bureaucracy. That bureaucracy which was a feature of British life so many decades ago has been inherited, preserved intact, embellished and developed. Indeed, everywhere are relics of those colonial days: preserved with affection and lack of rancour.

The island of Sri Lanka frequently gives the impression that very little has actually changed since the British left more than fifty years ago in 1948. Admittedly, they did change the name in a fit of socialist fervor, but the great institutions, like the army, still use Ceylon in their nomenclature. The army still uses British mess kit and customs, and bases its organisational structure on that of the British army.

In an article in *The Island* a Mr Chandraprema demonstrated a way with words and a certain understanding of the Sri Lankan army. Writing of Major General Waidyaratne, who died in December 2001, he affirms that he 'came from the English speaking, cricket and rugger playing, beer guzzling, whiskey (*sic.*) drinking, club going, ballroom dancing brown-Englishman class in Colombo. In the good old days, the Army was one of the proudest institutions of this class . . . He drank Scotch, ate bacon and eggs, and laced his conversations with many 'f's and 'b's. The kind of "rugger-bugger" esprits (*sic.*) de corps inculcated by the British army . . .'

Many business names are clearly inherited from a pre-independence past. Colonial Motors now sells (for the moment at least) Korean-built Kias rather than Landrovers, although the Defender remains the vehicle of choice for the elite police Special Task Force. Cinemas still sport names like The Regal, Dominion or Majestic. Buckingham Tailors may have recently closed its doors to give way to an internet and communications bureau, and nearby Hyde Park might now be a hangout for prostitutes and drug peddlers, but there is no inclination to actually change the names.

British royalty is written of in the newspapers in the sort of reverential tones the British press last used around the time of the Coronation. In amongst the adverts for Lifebuoy toilet soap and Rinso washing powder, a correspondent reminisced fondly in the local *Sunday Times*, "In the good ole days of British Colonial rule, we lived in peace, enjoying plenty of cheap bread and butter . . . the good ole days will never dawn again . . . [when] the Police Band was a must for all fashionable society functions and weddings and when the curtain fell they would play *God Save the King*".

When HRH The Prince of Wales visited the country in 1998 the vulgar British press pack accompanying the Prince scrutinised every blink, analysed every phrase uttered and interpreted every gesture. Any apparent infractions on the Prince's part were ruthlessly reported to eager readers back home. Additionally, there was a tasty story going the rounds about Arthur C Clarke and his alleged sexual peccadilloes: although they proved to be untrue, it gave the press much room for idle speculation.

The word used most frequently of HRH by the local press was 'charming'. Local media was highly critical when the Leader of the Opposition was bold enough to criticise the visit in advance. The general view was that this was simply a churlish way to attempt to score political points.

An advance press party had sneaked into the country on tourist visas ahead of the Prince's visit. Encamped at the Lanka Oberoi Hotel, they set about entrapping writer and guru Arthur C Clarke, who was due to receive his knighthood from the royal visitor. A Sunday tabloid broke allegations of Clarke's alleged paedophilia on its front page with the result the ceremony was cancelled.

When Charles then shook hands and spoke with Arthur C Clarke at the State Banquet at the President's House, the representatives of the British tabloid press went into a flat spin. The correspondent for the London tabloid *The Sun* could be heard barking down the hotel lobby phone to copytakers in London, "Catchline Perv, Prince shakes hands with alleged sex pervert . . .". This sort of conduct is distasteful and mystifying to people in a former colonial country which adheres to the old values rather more rigorously than the Brits now do; the people who like to think they invented those values. The prince's meeting with Arthur C Clarke did not receive one single column inch in any Sri Lankan newspaper the next day. My friend Gamini Werrakoon, editor of *The Island*, said he simply didn't regard it as newsworthy. By standards long forgotten in Britain that was probably a pretty fair assessment.

On the Thursday evening, the Prince made his way around the shady, treed garden at Westminster House, the British High Commissioner's large and opulent home in Colombo's poshest suburb. Apart from the human relics of British colonialism, in their fading, shabby tropical whites, there were gathered the Sri Lankans who do business with Britain: the women glittering in their saris, their husbands cool and smooth in sober, dark suits. For these locals, the opportunity to meet Prince Charles was accepted graciously and with gratitude. There was undiluted admiration for his resolve to come to their country in the face of terrorist threats.

There's no doubt. When the chips are down, the Prince of Wales - and, for that matter, several other members of the Royal family - are the longest serving and best ambassadors Britain has left. At home, we may think that we are rather too sophisticated to tolerate the Royals without constant, searching criticism. Out in the former colonies people aren't that sophisticated . . . or are they?

There are still a few tangible links with a colonial past which, far from being regretted, are looked back on with some affection. The GFH is not the only post-colonial hotel to survive in what used to be known as Ceylon. The Grand Oriental Hotel in Colombo used to be known as the Taprobane and was opened in 1837 to accommodate travelers arriving by sea. It has not managed to preserve the ancient colonial atmosphere as well as the GFH although its top floor restaurant has a wonderful panoramic view of the port of Colombo (no photographs allowed, for security reasons).

The Mount Lavinia Hotel is half an hour's drive south from Colombo. The original building on the site was the residence of the British Governor, Sir Thomas Maitland. Here, it is often said, he lived with his mistress: the English used to refer sniffily to that as 'going native'. The story goes that the lady was a bare breasted *mestizo* dancer named Lovina, an exotic local find for a British governor far from the chill of Scotland. When Maitland left the island in 1811, his house at Mount Lavinia, reputedly named after the lady, remained empty until the arrival of Governor Sir Edward Barnes who lavished much care, cash and attention on the property, extending and improving it.

The Mount Lavinia, along with the GFH, is one of the great colonial relics of old Ceylon. Once merely the weekend residence of the Governor, it is said that he was obliged by the British government to sell the magnificent retreat once they found out about it. In London, apparently, they failed to appreciate the luxury and expense of this remarkable piece of colonial architecture with its palatial rooms and labyrinthine corridors. It became a hotel in 1877. Today, it is fully modernised and represents the apogee of luxury. Barnes also was responsible for the construction of a very substantial residence in Nuwara Eliya – a favourite weekend retreat for

Colombo's rich and powerful rulers. That residence is now the Grand Hotel.

It is particularly agreeable to sit on the terrace at the side of the pool at the Mount Lavinia of a Sunday lunchtime as the bathers splash, a band plays and waiters in black tie serve ice-cold beers. The hotel stands on a promontory surrounded by the Indian Ocean on three sides and the uncanny impression, as a clarinettist plays *As Time Goes By*, is one of being on a luxury liner at sea. *Newsweek* magazine once described it as 'one of the world's best Gathering Places' and opined, 'For many people the romance of the East is inseparable from the old world charm of its colonial era buildings – and none is more romantic than Colombo's Mount Lavinia Hotel.'

The New Oriental Hotel in Galle, two hours drive from Colombo to the south of the island, was not still in the same league when it closed for renovations in 2002. Once it was the principal hotel in the picturesque fortified, walled town successively occupied by the Portuguese, the Dutch and the Brits. It is said to be the oldest registered hotel on the island, run by the Dutch burger Brohier family since 1899. The NOH, as it is known, is located in a building dating back to 1684 and which once served purpose as the British army barracks.

It was in a distinctly decayed condition when I stayed in the spring of 2001. The rooms were cavernous and rundown. In my room there were two four poster beds, a three piece art deco suite with tattered 1960s coverings and a ceiling fan with blades the size of an aircraft propeller. The colonial heritage was suggested by the pictures on the wall. There were two framed pictures of wrinkled, Dutch pipe-smoking fishermen on a beach in the Low Countries and matching pictures of our own Dear Queen and Prince Philip: colour pictures from the era of the coronation now turning a sickly green in the tropical sunlight. There was no air conditioning and the only protection against the depredations of the mosquitoes was a holed and grubby net around the four-poster. The hotel closed the following year for the injection of millions of Far Eastern investment from the hotel magnate Adrian Zeccha; now the faded grandeur was to be a thing of the past and that $350 room rate was well on the way.

A few years ago, the guidebooks noted the Dutch colonial furniture, the grand piano which guests were encouraged to play, and the Old Masters on the wall. The grand piano is still in evidence but nobody played it while I was staying. Apart from myself, there was a retired English couple who return year after year and an English film actor, one Oliver Tobias, on his honeymoon. He was a sort of Oliver Reed character here with his exceedingly beautiful young bride. The only film I can recall seeing him in, appropriately enough, was *The Stud*. I am glad to report he still seems to be lasting the pace. "I made a film here twenty years ago," he recalls nostalgically in the bar over a local Lion beer. "The army lent us five thousand men and an elephant-borne regiment of cavalry." Those days are long gone – as are the Old Masters and the best of the antique furniture.

But the place no visitor with a penchant for the delightfully archaic should miss is the 122 year-old Hill Club at Nuwara Eliya, in the centre of the island's tea growing area. High in the hills, it is cool and the weather frequently dismal. A bit like Scotland, really. The building itself is a cross between a Tudor castle and a Cotswold manor. Here, for around £30 a night, you can wander through a forgotten world of billiard tables, book-lined rooms, Men Only bars, and a withdrawing room with a wedding picture of Charles and Di still occupying pride of place as late as 1996.

Reassuringly, for a visitor from Scotland, over the stone fireplace in my bedroom there was a reproduction of Sir David Wilkie's sternly didactic *The Reading of the Will*. Jacket and tie were *de rigueur* at dinner until very recently but if you were caught short a member of staff would lead you to a wardrobe off the butler's pantry. There you could select from a range of soup-stained old school ties and butlers' jackets which would be duly handed back at the end of the evening. Now you can get away without a tie: a disappointing emergence into the 21st century. That notwithstanding, as soon as you reach your room, your own butler will arrive with a hot water bottle.

In the morning I was chuffed to leave with a monogrammed ashtray, a wonderfully stylish egg cup, the teapot and a candle holder stashed in my suitcase.

Sign of the times, old boy. They were flogging the china off at reception . . .

Bombs and dance floor shoutouts ...

I suppose the thing I really love about the GFH is that something is *always* going on. It is the port of call of the originals of this world: the eccentrics, the characters, the simply lunatic. At the very heart of the city, on the edge of Galle Green, it is at the epicentre of events. They are not always, of course, the sort of events you might voluntarily choose to be a participant in ...

It's virtually the only reasonable hotel in Colombo not to have been bombed by the Tamil Tigers, or LTTE as they are known in the contracted form for The Liberation Tigers of Tamil Eelam. The Intercontinental, now known as the Ceylon Continental, was bomb damaged in January 1996; the Galadari twice and the Hilton twice also, thanks to proximity to the Fort business district. The Indian showpiece hotel, the Taj Samudra, is too close for comfort to Army Headquarters, itself previously a target for the bombers. And so, before I came on my first visit back in January 1996, I asked the LTTE representative in London if I would be safe from his organisation's depredations at the GFH. He was reassuring. "Oh, I don't think we shall bother to blow up the Galle Face Hotel. Eventually, it will simply fall down of its own accord . . ." However, they did, in the event, lay on a most impressive show to mark my very first visit ...

It was almost a quarter to eleven on the morning of Wednesday January 31 in the teeming business quarter of the Sri Lankan capital, Colombo: a warm and overcast 31 degrees. Two vehicles were closing on the main thoroughfare, travelling separately from the east: a trishaw, the open three-wheeler transport so popular locally, and a large yellow, wooden-sided lorry ostensibly piled with 40 bags of rice husks. They were synchronised to meet up beyond the roundabout at the bottom of the street, between the *deluxe* Intercontinental Hotel and its neighbour the 4-star Galadari.

Opposite the forecourt of the Intercontinental, two men left the trishaw with short cylindrical bundles under their arms. The lorry, registration mark 42-6452, stopped in the clearly marked 'Towing Zone' at the front entrance of the Central Bank next to the security barrier. Immediately, security guards in light-brown coloured uniforms, armed with ancient single barrel 12-bore shotguns, stepped forward to move the truck on but, as they did so, two men dressed in traditional *sarongs* leapt from their positions perched on sacks of rice in the back of the truck. Both opened fire with Chinese manufactured T-56 5.6mm. semi-automatic rifles scattering the security guards.

Meantime, the two men from the trishaw had reached the Ceylinco Building, twenty or thirty yards down the road and the headquarters of the country's principal insurance company. As the commotion started at the bank across the road, security guards came running from the building and, in a planned diversionary tactic, one of the trishaw attackers unwrapped his bundle to reveal it to be a single-use, disposable rocket launcher, manufactured in Singapore. He shouldered and launched a missile through a window on the third floor of the building, which ignited almost immediately and flames leapt from the window.

Meantime, across the road, the driver of the lorry was repeatedly ramming the barrier at the front of the bank, reversing back and then trying again. This went on for fully three minutes. Police in the area took cover as soon as the fighting started, security guards fled, and, initially, although guards from the nearby Navy Headquarters building engaged the terrorists in fire, they also retreated after two of their number were shot and killed. They then took up defensive positions within the headquarters building, believing it to be under attack.

Unable to break through into the main foyer of the building, the driver left his cab in the *melee* at the front of the building, detonated an electric charge fixed to his 'suicide jacket' and blew the lorry's cargo: an estimated minimum of 400 kgs of

High Explosive, and possibly as much as 1,000. He was instantly buried under the collapsing frontage of the building.

Another terrorist had meantime been cut down by machine gun fire from the navy building and two of the others had made off in the trishaw. As the remaining three left the area, the blast of the explosion destroyed every single building on both sides of the road, the length of the main street of the commercial quarter: some 300 yards of frontage and twelve major buildings were destroyed in the explosion. All around the interiors of the buildings caught fire as electrics shorted, cars, trishaws and vans burned; almost a hundred people had died, either crushed by rubble or burned alive.

I looked at my watch as the massive explosion rocked the Sri Lankan capital of Colombo. It was 1047. I could see, through my car window, the plume of thick black smoke which was rising hundreds of feet into the air just a few hundred yards away.

Security that morning had been exceptionally tight throughout the city. Of course, that came as no great surprise: government forces had been pounding the separatist Tamil Tiger rebels in the north of the country since October 1995 and the big fear all along had been that in the wake of their defeat on their home territory in Jaffna, in the north of the country, they would bring the 13 year war, in which 50,000 had already died, to the country's capital.

Within minutes of the explosion Colombo seized up as army trucks, police, ambulances and rescue services converged on the commercial area. I abandoned my car, engaged a trishaw and then ran into a maelstrom of fire, debris and death.

In the area of the explosion in those minutes following it, visibility was reduced almost to zero. Thick black smoke billowed everywhere and through the thick, choking fog flames roared from windows, the heat searing your skin. On the edge of the commercial district, bedrooms in the ultra modern Intercontinental Hotel on the second and third floors were well alight: the service wing at the back was totally shattered and ablaze. On the forecourt of the hotel wandered a naked man - a German businessman - with just a bloody, once white bathroom towel wrapped around his waist. His face and body was shredded by shards of glass. He had just emerged from the shower when the explosion hit.

But I had seen nothing yet. The swirling blades of a circling Bell Huey 412 helicopter parted the black fog and I could see the length of the capital's main business street (its name translates to Presidential Street), buildings burning all the way along. The deluxe Galidari Hotel to my right had lost every single pane of glasss in its twelve storied facade. Next to it, the Ceylinco Insurance Company building, housing Ceylon's premier insurance company, was burning fiercely through its entire 12 stories or so. Next door, the building housing Air Lanka, the national carrier, was burning and it looked as though its floors had already collapsed. Further down the elegant colonial-style building of George Steuart's, the country's oldest trading company, was a shattered shell. But the worst hit was the Central Bank building, its modern green and white early '60s facade collapsed over pavement and road and with flames shooting through the rubble from underneath.

The street was an untidy mess of the detritus of war. There were the burned out cars. I counted more than thirty although, in fact, nearly 400 were wrecked, and trishaws - the small and noisy taxis you see everywhere - lay scattered all around. Curiously, the electrical effect of the explosion activated headlights and flashers and uselessly crushed and burned cars which would never run again winked and shone in seeming merry derision. And there was building rubble, glass and metal everywhere.

And the blood. In the 30 degree heat the blood was already dry on the pavements like pools of crimson sealing wax, quite hard and curiously less offensive than the blood I had seen in Bosnia, which always seemed so fresh and liquid.

All around milled the injured, the merely curious and the simply aimless. Police, army, navy and RAF personnel, Special

Task Force police, sailors in crisp white uniforms from the nearby Navy HQ, bomb disposal squads, commandos from the Airborne Division. There were even a few firemen. But turntable ladders and snorkels were not to arrive for more than an hour after the explosion and by one o'clock the Sri Lankan Air Force was dropping water bombs all over the blazing centre: Bell Huey helicopters scooping up water from the Beira Lake in front of the nearby parliament buildings and then dumping it in great curling showers from the sky.

All eyes at one point were turned to a window high up on the Ceylinco building. Two bloodied men, their clothes hanging in rags around them climbed onto the ledge of their window. You could see why: the flames shot out through the aperture behind them and they made to jump - just as part of the Central Bank collapsed behind me with a deep rumbling roar. Everybody sprinted for cover as debris showered down. I looked back at the window but the figures were gone. They had jumped.

A couple of hours later the police dug the body of one of the terrorists out of the rubble at the front of the bank. I've never seen a body quite like it. It immediately reminded me - rather ludicrously - of the bad taste joke about the man run over by a steamroller: they slipped him under the hospital door. This man no longer resembled an example of humanity: he was as flat as the proverbial pancake. "Tamil bastard," spat the policeman.

Seven hours later, as night fell in Colombo, smoke rose from the terminally shattered business heart of this Asian capital. A city centre curfew was imposed, there was a city wide appeal for blood donors and hospital staff, and the Department of Information was appealing for calm. 1400 people were admitted to the overworked hospitals and by nightfall the death toll was over 70.

From my room at the front of the GFH with its cracked panes, I could watch, as night fell, the smoke still rising into the sky. No time for a beer this evening. For me it would be a hectic evening and, indeed, right through the night I would be on the phone or at the computer. Fortuitously for journalists working in South Asia, the clock is eight hours ahead of Britain which gives plenty of time to gather news and then to file it during the evening hours. The deputy editor of *The Scotsman*, Fred Bridgland, urged me over the phone, "Give it all you've got, Paul. Bags of colour." It was next day's page one splash. Every three hours I did a live interview with the Sky News centre and they ran my voice over the powerful images which had come out of Colombo that day. In between I did interviews for BBC Radio Scotland's news programmes. This went on for three days, finishing with features for the Sunday papers.

A deep gloom settled over Colombo. The Tamil Tiger rebels had, in one blast, seriously undermined the commercial stability of Sri Lanka and done what they had long threatened by bringing war right into the heart of the capital.

***

I've never been much of a fan of breakfast: a meal to be approached circumspectly. My club, The Savile, in London has a most agreeable notice prominently displayed, *Talking Not Preferred*. Breakfast is a time for carefully taking stock of a day yet to start. Yet there is nowhere in the world, in my experience, where the start to the day can be as gentle and undemanding as on the terrace of the GFH.

It is December 2001. In some respects Christmas might be something to be practised on another planet. The morning paper reminds me that it is, indeed, Christmas. A columnist observes this morning, "There is a distinct nip in the air, Christmas is with us again . . ." The temperature outside is 28 degrees centigrade and the only nip in the air I can detect is that which occasionally wafts onto the naturally superheated balcony from the hotel air conditioning..

The ambient temperature may be three or four degrees below local expectations but it still seems decidedly hot and steamy. Below the terrace where I am taking breakfast, a solitary workman with an iron push-mower, circa 1950, works his way uncomplainingly across half an acre of rapidly grown grass. However, there is no denying that Christmas is here. The piped music displays a local enthusiasm for all the western favourites. *Winter Wonderland, Let it Snow* and *I'm Dreaming of a White Christmas* seem more than a little incongruous as the Indian Ocean waves gently break onto the beach just a few yards from the terrace in the shade of gently swaying palms. It seems all the more surprising that the enthusiasm for Christmas is so unrelenting around here.

In lifts, lobbies, hotel foyers, office buildings and shops of Colombo the Christmas message is all pervasive. White-bearded Santa Clauses with unmistakably brown features and wrapped presents stalk restaurants and hotels in search of small children. Christmas decorations and fairy lights illuminate the dingiest of Colombo's streets and the stalls of the pavement vendors are overflowing with plastic, inflatable Santas.

This is all vaguely perplexing in this overwhelmingly Buddhist country. Buddhism is enshrined in the constitution of Sri Lanka and Christians make up only around 10% of the population. Yet the Christmas message is universally embraced. Truth to tell, the Sri Lankans enthusiastically embrace every festival going: Valentine's Day, Father's Day, Easter, Halloween, the end of Ramadan, Buddhist full moon Poya days, the lot. They have more public holidays than any other country in the world, apparently.

This is part opportunism, part commercialism and part identification with Western culture. Despite years of war, there is still an extraordinary multi-culturalism which is unextinguished by years of ethnic war.

On Galle Face Green there has sprouted an illuminated message 'Peace on Earth'. When it went up at the beginning of December it seemed unconvincing against the backdrop of eighteen years of war with the LTTE, terrorist outrages and tens of thousands of deaths. But, following the December 5 election landslide and change of government there is undeniably an atmosphere of peace in the air even if a cooling of temperature is difficult to discern.

The LTTE grabbed the Christmas initiative on December 19 2001 with the announcement of a unilateral month long ceasefire in hostilities from midnight on December 24. It seemed highly likely that this 'unilateral' initiative had been brokered ahead of the election in secret talks with UNP representatives in the Vanni, north from Colombo The new United National Party government, determined to embrace the peace option, announced reciprocation of the ceasefire two days later. The following day, the new PM, Ranil Wickremesinghe, set off for New Delhi. It was widely anticipated that the new UNP government would go for negotiations with the LTTE through Norwegian so-called facilitators at the end of Christmas week, after Prime Minister Ranil Wickremesinghe returned from India, where he requested his counterpart Atal Biharee Vajpai to ensure India plays an active role.

The newspapers say the government is looking to Indian presence to strengthen the process so the rebels will stay committed to a negotiated settlement. And, like some enormous gift wrapped present, the economic embargo on rebel held areas in the north and east of the country is to be lifted on January 15.

All around Colombo, the night sky might not exactly be lit by the star of Bethlehem but there is the equally cheerful spark of oxy-acetylene cutting gear clearing away the metal barricades and checkpoints which have closed off whole areas of the city from traffic for up to seven years. Streets which have not seen a bus or a car or a three wheeler for years, as the city went into siege mode against the threat of suicide bombers, now teem with traffic.

The practical matter of facilitation of movement is appreciated all around. Everybody talks excitedly of how quickly they can get from home to office, from shopping mall to home, from wife to lover, even. But it is the simple feeling of optimism which this simple gesture has engendered which is probably the most hopeful development. It somehow seems the most tangible of moves towards a peace that has always been elusive. It seems churlish to point out, especially at Christmas, that previous ceasefires have a history of irretrievably breaking down once both sides in the conflict have regrouped and rearmed and the talking has petered out. Jaw-jaw has always been replaced by war-war. But, if Christmas is about hope then this must be the one time of the year that dreams might be cherished.

On Christmas Day the newspapers are published as normal in Colombo. The journalists have their day off on Christmas Day itself which means no papers on the 26th – an eminently sensible arrangement. Although the front pages are dominated by predictions of island-wide peace and harmony, page three of *The Island* reveals a rather darker side to things. A fifty-year-old father of five "who was an active supporter of the People's Alliance committed suicide by swallowing poison as the PA was defeated at the parliamentary election." A farmer has committed suicide by swallowing poison because "one of his enemies had filled water into his paddy fields which had been prepared for sowing the following day." Sri Lanka has, in fact, the highest rate of suicide in the world. Somewhere else a village woman overcome by coping with the drunkenness of her husband has jumped into a well together with her baby.

The mode of expression in the local papers is frequently coy, if not downright quaint. The *Daily News* advises, "Ratnapura police arrested a foreign woman on a charge of practising the oldest profession in the world in a guest house at Batagadera." Apparently, hordes of Russian hookers have penetrated even the remotest parts of Sri Lanka.

Elsewhere there is news of power cuts to come in a country with a dangerous lack of electricity generating capacity. At the bottom of page three, there is news of another shortage. "Almost all post offices in the Badulla district are short of stamps of all denominations . . . meanwhile the machine used for stamp sealing is so worn that nothing appears, not even the date."

***

Sanjeev Gardiner, Chairman of the Galle Face Hotel, tells me cheerfully and confidently that New Year's Night is "the great night" for the GFH. He wasn't exaggerating . . . but his father Cyril would assuredly have thought differently.

There has been ample evidence of preparation for days. The seafront patio with its chequerboard of white and black tiles is the focus of activity. A rectangular steel gantry surrounding the space has been erected and the cross members are now sprouting lights and wiring. A roofed dais has grown at the side and mixers, speakers and all manner of technical paraphernalia is in evidence with 24 hours to go.

Tables, chairs and tented areas spread like mushrooms across the garden overlooking the sea and by mid-afternoon on the 31st the preparations for bacchanalia are complete. Shortly before 5 p.m. the heavens open and the tropical downpour starts: seemingly solid sheets of rain soaking tablecloths, overflowing gutters and filling upturned cups. Forty-five minutes later it is over as suddenly as it started.

For Colombo's *jeunesse d'ore* the opportunity of seeing in the New Year in the unique seafront surroundings is the hottest ticket in town. Sold out weeks ago at three and a half thousand rupees a go (US$ 40), tickets were on the black market at twice the price a week ago. Five hundred, officially, of the local beautiful people sat down to dinner under the stars. Some say that more than a thousand tickets were sold. Braziers burned on the seafront, under the 19th century illuminated façade, flashing lights and disco and live rock music reverberated through the structure of the ancient building, the base notes vibrating through teak floorboards, ill-fitting window panes and balcony doors.

From nine in the evening the chauffeur driven four wheel drives deposited Colombo's rich and the beautiful: men booted and suited, an unusual sight here where open neck shirts are more often *de rigeur*, and the girls in their modern, elegant, figure-hugging designer clothes. The girls represent a sort of perfection as it is perceived here with their perfect, pale skins. Many of them would easily pass for white European women; they would like that, if you might point it out. Many of the darker skinned women who arrive are, well, here for the enjoyment of others rather than themselves . . .

A sparkling white Lexus four-wheel drive, US$150,000 worth of luxury imported motor car if import duties are paid, arrives at the portico. Another ostentatious machine in metallic red bears the name of the Italian fashion house 'Prada' painted on the side like two go-faster stripes. It decants two couples and their 'protection': a group of well-built youths with loose shirts. The girls are obvious and sexy rather than beautiful. For gangsters' molls the fashion seems to be for the short cocktail dress worn tight like some reptilean second skin.

One such vehicle – from a fleet of ten soon to be parked in serried ranks before the open portico - deposits the son of a government minister, S B Dissanayake. Young Taraka is not only in the possession of the hottest ticket in town, he has also booked the vast Royal Suite for his own bash. He has a posse of MSD goons – Ministerial Security Department close protection agents – who are equipped with pistols, tucked into the waistbands of their trousers, hidden by the long, baggy white shirts favoured by close protection security men around here. The girls in his party are light-skinned, lissom and lithe. All the assets in place. But, as a Sunday newspaper, would ungallantly point out, Taraka's girlfriend failed all her 'O' Levels.

The GFH is divided from Galle Green by Kollupitiya Road, a once private road owned by the hotel when it was built in the 19th century. The modest width of the road might as well be an unbridgeable chasm for those celebrating on the Green. For Galle Green is where those with no other place of recreation flock with their firecrackers and rockets in their best, frayed frocks and ill fitting Sunday best. They may come from Colombo's spreading slums but they are dressed to celebrate in as much style as they can muster, arriving in the ubiquitous three wheelers: noisy pollutants of the atmosphere but cheap family transport.

Intriguingly, there is scarcely an envious glance from the *hoi polloi* on the Green in the direction of the capital's high society. They are inured to the opulence; to the fact of life that most in society will be poor and that just a very limited few will achieve inconceivable heights of affluence and position. Both seemingly carry on life oblivious of the other.

The two groups are discreetly separated by khaki-clad police with T-56 semi-automatic weapons . . . just in case. But their presence is hardly necessary. A group of boys, maybe fifteen or sixteen years old, do gather at one point to stare at the arrivals as if they are rolling up for a Hollywood Oscar ceremony. But this *salon de refuses* looks more bemused than envious. Just a few do try to get in later but they will *not* go to the ball. The premises are secured by dozens of uniformed private security men who ruthlessly turn away the unwelcome. Their success in this will, of course, be rather dented in the early hours of the morning . . .

Virtually everyone arriving at the GFH seems to be talking animatedly on a cellphone. One cool dude at a dinner table below a vast spreading palm on the hotel's seafront is jabbering into a cellphone held firmly in one hand. His other hand is firmly lodged up his girlfriend's minidress. Such is the nature of communication at the beginning of the 21st century.

Shortly after midnight it is not all tidings of joy. A young fellow on his own with his shirt open to his navel and sporting a hairy chest is proclaiming into his 'phone, "I'm sick of all your crap, your stomach turning nonsense . . ." The rest of the diatribe is lost as he moves into the jostling heart of the party.

How on earth telephonic communication is achieved against the deafening competition from the discotheque is a mystery. It is clear, however, that the cellphone doubles as a modern social support mechanism. For a girl without a dance left at the dinner table there is the phone for sustenance, as a means to pre-empt social embarrassment. Then when a suitable male appears it is promptly popped back into a bag or pocket.

The offspring of cabinet minister S B Dissanayake, Taraka, is your archetypal poor little rich kid. He has been banned from at least one of the capital's five star hotels and is a well practised troublemaker. Refused entry to a cricket match, he famously declared that unless he was admitted his father would declare the result null and void. He was admitted . . . Tonight he is in full flow.

The sight of a former girlfriend dancing with some other fellow fazes the prominent guest completely. The girls fight and the fur flies as hair is pulled, skin is bitten and clothes torn. Goons are called up to sort matters out as the VIP goes berserk beating his former girlfriend, smashing chairs, tables and glasses. Attempts to restrain the fellow by fellow celebrants occasions what will become infamous as the Galle Face New Year Fracas. The goons are now on site, having forced their way in, clubbed security men and hotel receptionist alike with their pistol butts. Now they fire their weapons, 'sending the glitzy revellers running helter skelter', as one Sunday paper would put it, and causing the disc jockey to call out desperately for assistance. "Security to the dance floor, security to the dance floor . . ." The melee worsens. According to one newspaper correspondent – 'A Disgusted Reveller' – "He and his gang were throwing chairs, overturning tables, breaking bottles and glasses. . . The fight gradually moved to the car park of the hotel, by which time the garden where the dance was taking place looked like a war zone. It's time we all got together and said, NO MORE!'

In fact, when assistance does come – in the form of a couple of dozen police waving T-56 semi-automatic assault rifles – it is clear who they have pitched up to protect. There is apparently no complaint for them to act upon, and they rapidly depart having assured themselves that the 'VIP's' life is not in danger. As *The Sunday Leader* puts it 'old habits die hard', despite a rather new, three week old government apparently dedicated to upholding the rule of law. The Sunday newspapers will make great play of the incident which will become a veritable *cause celebre*. In one newspaper, the incident will feature as a page one story, dominate the letters page and constitute the subject matter for an editorial headed The New Year Fracas. According to the leader in *The Sunday Island*, "security details assigned to politicians have been converted to virtual private armies and hit squads." Within days this is being referred to gravely as 'the Galle Face Hotel incident'. On television the newly appointed Minister of the Interior blithely avers that it is the responsibility of hotel security (unarmed) to ensure that people with firearms (i.e. armed) do not enter social events on their premises. In fact, the scion of an important clan advised a security man who blocked him that if he ever saw him again he was dead. The poor chap did not pitch up to work the next day.

A local business magnate will feel obliged, ten days later, to take quarter page advertisements in the main Sinhala and English newspapers 'to inform the General Public that a news item . . . of an incident that took place at the Galle Face Hotel during the New Year's Eve dance highlighting the persons involved in the incident as being daughters of Salaka magnate (*sic*) . . . The said persons referred to on the news item are not my daughters and I disassociate myself, my family, and my business ventures as having any connection what so ever (*sic*) with the said incident, and the said persons.' With blanket press coverage, government ministers commenting and police investigations one might be forgiven for opining things have got slightly out of hand. But serious issues have been raised at the very start of the term of office of a new government and a new Prime Minister professing to uphold a battered and bleeding rule of law.

Should the children of ministers be entitled to armed security provided by the State? Why was nobody arrested in connection with the incident? Was the police response a trifle selective? Whose weapon was actually used and was it licensed? One newspaper report suggests that there are more than 20,000 unlicensed weapons in circulation after nineteen years of war, many supplied by thousands of deserters from the armed forces, and a seemingly inextinguishable gun culture. Just before the December election, one Sunday newspaper recounted an incident in a Colombo nightclub when a son of the Deputy Defence Minister, Anuruddha Ratwatte, entered the club with his guards, cronies and hangers on. The manager sent out word with a waiter that the party was too large and would he please leave? He took his pistol from his waistband, emptied the magazine and placed a single bullet on the waiter's tray. "Ask your manager if he would prefer to have this inside him," was the riposte.

Having wreaked havoc – 'played the devil' as one daily newspaper quaintly puts it – the VIP removed himself to the King Emperor suite – the largest sitting room in any suite in any hotel in the world, according to the GFH, and continued to party there. together with ten girls, by all accounts.

Nobody would ever be prosecuted for causing the fracas, discharging weapons, injuring guests, assaulting staff and smashing hotel property. Regrets were expressed, privately. The alleged perpetrator was called to the local police station to apologise to staff from the GFH, and his father apologised to his boss, the Prime Minister. As one observer put it, "It's only in a banana republic, like ours, that one can get away with a serious crime by apologising to the Prime Minister . . . The failure of the police to apprehend the culprit and indict him means only one thing: it is the degeneration of the new UNP government within one month of coming to power."

Indeed, The Honorable Ranil Wickremesinghe was, according to Cabinet sources, extremely put out by the incident – actually the first political crisis of his term of office which had started but three weeks or so earlier. But the police chose to deal with it in the usual relaxed manner they are accustomed to handling the offences of politicians and the powerful. Seemingly everybody has anecdotes involving the avoidance of penalty for acts of violence ranging from a former Cabinet Minister's son shooting someone dead in a casino in front of dozens of witnesses, to running a hapless pedestrian over outside. During 2002, there would be a seemingly endless series of assaults and discharge of lethal weapons in five star hotels in Colombo. The most popular location for such 'high spirits' would be the Blue Elephant nightclub below the Hilton Hotel, although the single most bloody incident would take place in October at the Trans Asia as a UNP businessman celebrated a deal to privatise the country's buses: management, staff and guests would be beaten to pulp in the foyer of the hotel by black-garbed, machine gun wielding private 'security guards'. No prosecutions would follow.

At eight in the morning on January 1 2002, two hours after dawn, three or four dozen indomitable survivors still dance to the relentless beat of the disco.. The men are decidedly worse for wear, their shirts stained by the sweat of their all night exertions. Amazingly, the girls still appear fresh and fragrant, their expensive clothes pristine and crisp in the gentle, early morning light. In mini-dresses, slit skirts and glittering outfits with halter tops in constant need of adjustment, they dance insouciantly amidst the debris of broken chairs, smashed glasses, discarded paper plates and spent bullet casings.

In the hill country, four or five hours drive away from the capital, the women laborers on the tea estates had already begun their first working day of the year by cutting the throat of a goat and smearing the machines in the tea factory with its blood. For them, at least, this will, traditionally, be their insurance for a year free of accidents. The machines of the factory will not claim *their* blood this new year.

Weddings & Beauty Queens

The newspapers are entertaining and breakfast on the terrace is distinctly enlivened by their appearance. There are three English language dailies. *The Daily News* is the government paper, religiously toeing the official line. When the UNP government was elected in December 2001, a vitriolic campaign of hate, propaganda and malicious rumor ceased overnight. The previous days' masters in the PA government instantly became the objects of venom in an extraordinary turnaround. This at least livened up for a few days what is essentially a propaganda sheet with strictly limited entertainment value. Its Sunday stable mate, *The Sunday Observer*, shares the same turncoat propensity and was positively lauding the former opposition in its first issue after the election.

The Island is a rather different kettle of fish. Fiercely critical of the government of the day, it somehow manages to tread the narrow line between criticism and causing offence which some other newspapers – particularly *The Sunday Leader* and *Sunday Times* – have failed to do, and ended up in the courts in the past for their troubles. Press freedom is a delicate plant in Sri Lanka and more than one editor has died violently in recent years, others have been shot at and beaten up, and the odd one thrown into jail.

Chairman and publisher of *The Sunday Leader* Lal Wickrematunge told me over coffee on the terrace of the GFH a few years ago, "We started on a shoestring budget buying one computer a month." A year later, they bought a printing press in the United States for $50,000. By the beginning of 1996, he claims, *The Leader* had overtaken the government *Sunday Observer* and the pro-opposition *Sunday Island* to become the second largest, after *The Sunday Times*.

Said Chairman and publisher Lal then, "We are against the government so we are tagged as supporting the UNP (opposition party). But we don't see ourselves as being politically aligned. Our success has been in investigative reporting." The paper uncovered a series of scandals involving senior government figures. It has revealed a minister as having his personal credit card accounts paid by the chairman of a recently privatised telecommunications company. Similarly, it found that the newly privatised national airline Air Lanka had purchased Airbus aircraft at costs in excess of the list price. It found that the President did not have the qualification she claimed from the Sorbonne as an economist. When they uncovered this matter the editor wrote a personal letter to the president apprising her of the outcome of the investigation. Her senior assistant secretary wrote back tartly advising, "Only letters from human beings are submitted to the President and not from worms. Accordingly, your letter will be consigned to the rubbish heap." As counsel for *The Sunday Leader* pointed out in court, "It is a matter of shame for this country that such a letter is sent to the editor of a national newspaper."

Editor Lasantha Wickrematunge and his wife were returning home from the office in 1997 and were pulled from their car by masked gunmen who emerged from an unmarked vehicle. They were beaten with nailed clubs and both were hospitalised with severe injuries. The crime was not solved by the police. Two years later, they were parking their car outside their home and were about to enter the house together with their children aged six months, six and eight years and masked gunmen opened fire on them with automatic weapons. The police found 48 spent government-issue T-56 rounds at the scene. No arrests were made. This attack was in the aftermath of the exposure of the alleged involvement of one of the President's friends and advisers in the purchase of radio and television licences.

On May 8 2000, the government gazetted emergency regulations to censor both national and international press operating on the island. On April 28, there had been a severe reverse in the war with the Tamil Tigers in the north of the island as the strategic Elephant Pass military complex fell and government forces went into retreat. On May 9, the so-called Competent Authority, Information Department head Arya Rubesinghe, wrote to the *Leader* drawing its attention to information published "in the recent past" on May 7, before the regulations were announced.

On May 21, *The Sunday Leader* published an article entitled 'War in Fantasyland'. Heavy on irony, this reported that government troops were not under pressure in the Jaffna Peninsular and that they were not sustaining heavy casualties. It effectively reported the situation by denying events. Response from the Competent Authority came the next day. Around 100 police arrived in trucks and sealed the press. A 24-hour police guard was placed on the *Leader* premises and the Competent Authority served notice that the paper that it would be closed for a period of six months and that the press would be sealed. Other publications produced under contract at its plant would effectively be banned.

Whilst the PA was in government the *Leader* successfully nurtured its image as a campaigning, fearless newspaper. With the election of the UNP in December 2001, it was startlingly transformed, overnight, into the mouthpiece of the new government; lapdog of the new prime minister, Ranil Wickremesinghe.

The latest appearance on the newspaper market then was *The Daily Mirror*. It was altogether lighter, brighter and better laid out than its daily rivals. But reading all of the daily papers you get the impression there can't be a copy or sub-editor in sight. The same story frequently appears in two or, even three, places in the same edition; misprints abound; stories allegedly continued on another page frequently don't; and some of the language used is positively quaint to a reader from abroad. Bank robberies are 'heists'; detectives are 'sleuths'; a navy patrol apprehends smugglers in 'the wee hours of the morning'; suspects aren't arrested, they are, rather, 'nabbed' and accident victims are 'warded' rather than hospitalized. There is much talk of 'goon squads'. A strike at a hospital brings the headline 'Docs down Steths'. The French word *sans* has somehow crept into usage in place of the English word 'without'.

Apparently, there are sub-editors eking out a living in the bowels of the newspapers. Vijitha Yapa, erstwhile journalist and editor and now the largest bookseller in the country, tells the story of when he was editing *The Island*. The coroner from some remote country district telephoned him to ask why the paper had announced his premature death in a news story. A local doctor had committed suicide and the coroner had duly recorded the circumstances but somehow the suicide had been wrongly ascribed to the coroner. Vijitha tackled the sub editor on the matter who cheerfully volunteered the information, "I couldn't believe that a doctor – a rich man – would commit suicide. I thought it was far more likely that the coroner – a poor man – would do this so I changed the story around."

On another occasion, Vijitha had a bad feeling about the next day's paper. He couldn't put his finger on what was disturbing him so went by the office as the paper went on the machine. To his horror he found the headline relating to the President's admonition of a political colleague, Finance Minister Ronnie de Mel, appearing as PRESIDENT DENIES HE RAPED RONNIE, rather than the rather less inflammatory 'rapped'. On another occasion, another paper advises its readers in its headline that a certain official had been stripped by his Minister. Relieved of office, certainly, but not unclothed. Then we learn 'Suicide Bomber Blows Himself' and a sports writer, skilled in the art of the mixed metaphor, tells us 'The Indian team capsized like a pack of cards'.

But it's the stuff that emanates from the remoter provinces which is sometimes amusing, sometimes tragic and often bizarre. At the beginning of January, an extraordinary tale of a hapless headmistress and her appointment with death emerged from a remote part of eastern Sri Lanka and was featured on the front page of *The Sunday Observer*.

Forty year-old Mrs Doreen Kulandaivelu was returning home to Pandiruppu from the school where she was a principal when her trailing *saree* became entangled in the rear wheel of her motorcycle. She fell from the motorcycle and was injured. Passers by despatched her in a three wheeler to hospital at nearby Kalmunai. Halfway there, however, the three wheeler engine failed and she was transferred to another three wheeler. The engine of that one also stalled a few miles from the hospital.

As her condition worsened she was put in a passing car and admitted to the hospital. But doctors decided to transfer her by ambulance to a larger hospital at the main town of Batticaloa. The ambulance, which was said to be travelling at high speed with its siren on, collided head-on with a van coming in the opposite direction. Five persons, including the ambulance driver and two medical staff, were seriously injured and all, including Mrs Kulandaivelu, were transferred to another vehicle. Upon arrival at Batticaloa Hospital Mrs Kulandaivelu was found to be dead. Surprise, surprise.

Another choice tale appeared in *The Island* of January 2. A man from the Matara area was arrested by the police on the complaint of a 23 year-old woman. Apparently, she had married a local fisherman and after seven days of marriage her spouse went off to sea on a fishing trip. As the newspaper put it, 'For some reason or other he did not return for several months. . .' She came to know a 45 year-old man who was said to be a *kapumahattaya* in a *devale*. 'After hearing her sad story the *kapuwa* said he could bring back her husband in seven days.' For that purpose she should come to his *devale*. When she arrived there he gave her a white cloth and told her to have a bath and come to him dressed in the white cloth . . . 'She obliged and when she appeared before him she was told to lie down at a certain place in the *devale*. Thereafter he had raped her.

'After a few days her husband had returned home. Then she had told her husband everything about the rituals she had conducted. The fisherman, who realized what had taken place, went to the Matara police along with his wife and lodged a complaint.'

Unfair, or what? Shades of *The Rainmaker* . . .

Other slices of life prompt the query as to what on earth is going on in the nether regions of the country. A young woman 'posing off', as it is put, as a man, married a garment factory girl, after securing employment as a supervisor at the same factory in Kelaniya. Garment factory officials found out, however, and handed her over to the police.

A broadly similar problem emerged in Matara when a 20 year-old male with a history of swallowing poison was admitted to Ward 16 of Matara General Hospital. He was 'traced to be a female when an attempt was made to connect a catheter for passage of urine. On further tests, he was found to be she and not a he, carrying a three month old foetus . . .'

In Boosa, a man convicted of bigamy had a 'pleasant surprise' when the woman who sued him paid up the fine herself and took him home after mortgaging her jewellery. According to the Frauds Bureau of the Galle Police, the man concerned had felt ' lonely and heartbroken' when his wife went abroad for employment and married another woman, pretending to be a bachelor. 'After having a happy time with the second woman, he had reunited with the first wife the moment she returned on completion of her stint abroad.'

From Puttalam comes the 'astonishing news' of two youths of identical age suffering from an identical disability meeting with death in an identical manner. Irosha Lakmani (17) was deaf and dumb. On the 27th of May she was 'bathing from the water pouring down from a coconut tree in front of her house. Whilst bathing she was killed by lightning. Almost at the same time, another deaf and dumb youth of 17 – S Jayaratne – was bathing in the village tank with one of his friends when he too died after being struck by lightning.'

My favourite, though, was printed under the strap-head 'Only the dead can live with that noise' 'A resident of Borella, vexed by his neighbour's excessive nightly revelries, has decided to turn his luxury house into a modern crematorium cum funeral parlour and donate it to the poor living within the Colombo municipal limits. It is not known how soon the dear departed will be able to enjoy this great windfall.' *The Island* further explained that the resident 'had no choice but to invite the dead to move into his premises as his neighbour tormented him remorselessly with his revelries and explosive music . . . the neighbour is alleged to be a mega arms dealer who has made a fortune on the war. Once he was quoted in the local media saying: "I have many friends in politics and perhaps they are the best money can buy."

'The arms dealer's residence was once dubbed by the media as the Millennium Party Centre and is furnished with an outdoor bandstand . . .'

Tackled on the issue, said arms dealer responded to the effect that he did indeed enjoy good parties but only one neighbour complained. Said 'sick neighbour' had telephoned his wife and abused her. "A person who scolds a neighbour's wife cannot be on," he ventured.

The Mayor of Colombo confirmed he had been offered the land for a crematorium.

***

The Galle Face Green outside the hotel was restored at great expense, over a considerable period of time, following years of decline and reopened to the public as a recreation ground in September 2001. The repair and renovation, including newly planted grass, *palmyrah* trees and plants, cost some 70 million rupees; almost a million US dollars. In the years running up to the restoration of the turf, people had wryly been referring to it as Galle Face *Brown*. Although the grass had been refurbished on several occasions, it was never given time to recover before the public were unleashed on it again and those brown, bald patches grew ever larger. One local journalist claims that the decline started on Republic Day in 1972 when soldiers marched on the Green. At least it is no longer used as an emergency aircraft landing strip. It has, however, been turned over to everything from political gatherings to pop concerts. Its nadir came in 1999 when the army's tattoo to celebrate its 50th anniversary saw 200 armoured vehicles careering around the grass, ripping up the turf. In the following days it rained incessantly and turned the Green into a sea of mud.

The latest restoration has, to a large extent, also been frustrated by those who use the Green. A combination of heavy usage and insouciance means that maintenance is proving both costly and difficult. The Urban Development Authority has described it as 'a challenging test due to the unruly behaviour of the visiting crowds and their scant disregard to appeals to keep the Green clean . . . it has become extremely difficult to conserve the Green.' By the summer of 2002, the palmyrah trees lining the Green could be seen to be visibly wilting, the leaves turning a fragile brown. *The Daily News* put the problem down to the drought although an eminent horticulturalist averred that they were the wrong sort of tree to attempt to grow so near the destructive salinity of the sea.

Of a holiday, or a Sunday evening, the Green is thick with Colombo residents for whom it is variously simple green space, refuge and recreation ground. Cyril Gardiner once said his hotel enjoyed the "biggest parking lot in the world": the Green to the front, which was indeed formerly utilized for car parking, and the Indian Ocean which stretches westwards all the way to Somalia. For those on the Green, his hotel is a stern, remote place perhaps to be visited one day for a wedding. Journalist Bandula Jayasekera remembers in his youth, "The Galle Face Hotel stood tall but we never went near because we were worried that we'd end up washing plates." By night, the Green is noisy and vibrant, the darkness pierced by the fluorescent lights of mobile diners and fast food sellers. The warm night air is rendered fragrant by the smell of barbecued chicken, curry-in-a-hurry and *samosas*. Of a morning the green is a litter of broken bottles, discarded polythene bags, remnants of fast food takeaways. Early morning joggers and exercise freaks pick their way through the debris until it is retrieved by dark-skinned, frail looking Tamil women used by the private contractors to clear up after the excesses of the night before. Of a weekend, the range of activities is as diverse as the human condition: kite flying, donkey rides, cricket, football and the secret games of uncontrollable children.

Day or night, young lovers sit on the benches, holding hands, staring into each other's eyes. In the heat of the day, they crouch beneath umbrellas shaded from the sun and from the eyes of the curious. Of a morning, around seven or eight, the sun is but a watery yellow promise of the heat of the day to come. The umbrellas are neatly rolled. The lovers are dressed for the office. The men are in their neatly pressed black trousers; a shirt that doesn't quite make it into the executive wear league. The girls in saris, long frocks or long skirts always look infinitely more sartorial than their consorts. They also tend to look surprisingly unhappy. I am often driven to wonder as I jog around the Green of a morning if these are relationships made in heaven or illicit relationships formed beside the photocopier.

It was reported in the local press that a police constable from an outlying district was in the habit of extorting money from couples relaxing on the Green. Usually intimacy is coy, often furtive. In public, a head discreetly laid on a shoulder, a hand on a knee. Underneath the shelter of the umbrellas, a squeeze here, an intimate touch there. But this is a no kissing zone. Public affection is not an acceptable manifestation, even on the Green, the only place where thousands of young lovers can gather away from their humble dwellings in very public privacy. Carl Muller is said to have upset Colombo society with his novel *Colombo* and his frank and uncompromising descriptions of life on and around the Green. 'This was the Galle Face Green – a big, dust-skirted lung in a city of smoking buses and melting tar on hot roads and clogged, festering drains and whores outside the Hilton and the Inter-Continental and at the top of Baillie Street.' Muller has a keen eye for low life on the Green. 'Lives have been lost here, blood spilt, women gang raped, male prostitutes sodomized and addicts still stumble or stand, sniffing, nervously waiting for their suppliers.'

The events of the 1980s and 1990s, and the proximity of army headquarters and the Ministry of Defence, meant that security considerations might frequently impinge upon the carefree nature of the Green. Photography became an activity associated with a possible threat to the state. Even the most innocent of activities could be subject to censure. Revisiting the Green in December of 1999, as the millennium approached, Bandula Jayasekera 'walked up and down, went down memory lane and sat on a bench. A cop questioned me, "What are you doing here?" I answered, "I am thinking." He growled, "You can't think here".'

The Green was a familiar sight to the writer Arthur C Clarke who had been able to observe it on his many visits to the suite at the hotel where he worked on his books when life became too distracting at his Colombo home and office. In June 2002 there was a rash of UFO sightings, mainly in the east of Sri Lanka around Polonnaruwa. A sceptical Clarke, regarded as an eminent authority on sci-fi matters including such unexplained sightings, averred that most so-called UFOs were, in fact, IFOs: Identifiable Flying Objects. He pointed out that under certain weather or light conditions many objects in the night sky, such as Venus, the moon or meteors, might be mistaken as strange, alien objects. One report of a UFO was made by Jimmy Carter, who later became a President of the United States. The object turned out to be Venus.

Observed Clarke, "The Galle Face Green is a good place to see so-called UFOs. In the evening you can see a rich variety of objects in the sky – some natural, others man-made. With a little imagination, you can come up with a story that can easily get onto the front page. Perhaps that's exactly what laymen and scientists have been doing in recent days."

***

At the end of the 1960s, Cyril Gardner decided to 'kill' the wedding trade. Managing director Lalith Rodrigo recalls that Cyril blamed problems at the hotel on the disruption and noise caused by the lucrative wedding business, "In those days there were only three prestige hotels for weddings in Colombo. There was the Galle Face, the Grand Oriental and the Mount Lavinia. But, with Cyril, the hotel guests came first." To emphasise the point, he sold off half of the hotel's chairs as an insurance against his wishes not being observed. A rather solid chunk of business disappeared overnight.

It gradually crept back but a lack of chairs kept functions down to one at a time. "We had strict instructions never to hire things like chairs," recalls Rodrigo. By the late 90s, however, with Cyril's demise the weddings returned. "In many ways it was like *perestroika* in Russia. Things we hadn't been able to do for years came back." Prawns were served again. Cyril had forbidden them on the grounds that if anyone had a stomach upset they would always blame it on prawns, and he did not want the Galle Face blamed. He took a dislike to serving pork, as he wished not to offend visiting Muslims, and it also disappeared from the menu. He was known to chase away a waiter who tried to remove a soup bowl with a couple of spoonfuls left in the bottom: he abhorred waste.

Cyril had never allowed a bar in the hotel and, a couple of years after he died, one with stools to sit at sprouted on the terrace. A television even appeared in the corner but, thankfully, apart from when a cricket match was on, it remained clothed in a sheet most of the time. The swimming pool under CG was filled with brine: he was a great believer in its health giving, disinfectant properties. He used to say that the hotel had two swimming pools: the one on the terrace and the largest one in the world – the Indian Ocean.

However, the bar still remains closed on all the very many public holidays which Sri Lanka enjoys – more public holidays than any other country in the world. Holidays for Sinhalese – full moon Poya Days – and Muslim holidays like Idul Fitri are observed, as well as Tamil holidays like Thai Pongal, national Independence Day and World Temperance Day. Then it is virtually impossible to track down a drink in the hotel, although I have prevailed on waiters to serve me a beer from my own fridge poured into a teapot and served in a cup and saucer.

As one expatriate diplomat observed sniffily on a trip to the hotel, "This place is now a regular wedding palace." To my mind, they impart a distinctive and attractive local atmosphere to the place. For a few hours, it is filled with locals dressed to the nines. The women never fail to look glamorous in their *sarees*, despite the fact that in everyday life one might not give them a second look. The younger women look simply devastating. Not only does the local dress impart a traditional beauty, but there is also a natural grace about these dark-skinned beauties. There are sometimes as many as half a dozen weddings a day at the hotel. That is to say, when the day is an 'auspicious day', according to the Buddhist calendar. The Buddhist ceremonies are all civil proceedings presided over by a civil registrar. The register will be signed at a precise, auspicious time. That's fine when everybody is in place, but at one wedding attended by the Prime Minister he was a couple of hours late and the hapless couple missed their auspicious time – hopefully without long term consequences.

The weddings take place all over the hotel – sometimes simultaneously. In the Palm Lounge, the Jubilee Room, the

Grand Ballroom, on the terrace and on the patio of an evening. For Sri Lankans, the reputation of the GFH as 'the place' to be remains. Its colonial reputation as the premier hotel remains *virgo intacto*, so to speak. Just as in weddings all over the world, the ceremony is followed by food and by dancing. Also, just as everywhere else, the men sometimes peel off from the larger gathering. On the terrace I see a couple of dozen men group together and order a bottle of whisky (there is no alcohol served at the wedding party). A bottle of Johnnie Walker Red Label is deposited on the table by a waiter and they gulp it furtively. Johnnie Walker is popular around here and is, indeed, almost synonymous with whisky for many Sri Lankans. The truly discerning go for Black Label, but that is still only for the *cognoscenti*, given availability and price. As they are quaffing their Red, one of their wives arrives on the terrace and half a dozen of them bolt off. But there are always one or two of the unattached left to 'guard' the illicit refreshment . . .

***

This is not a beauty contest. Locally it is known as a *panchakalyani*. Last Sunday's paper advised that 'a *panchakalyani* queen, a true Sri Lankan beauty', will be chosen at the 'grand finals' at the GFH.

We are on the terrace of the GFH at lunch. The card says much about Mr Caldera. Apparently, he is Chairman and Director General of the Youth Foundation of Sri Lanka (200,000 members), in turn affiliated to the United Nations Youth & Student Organisation of Sri Lanka. Indeed, his card proudly bears the blue and white symbol of the United Nations. Impressive stuff.

Dr Sri Lal Caldera is the big cheese in the beauty queen business, apparently. Started in 1975, this is the fifth contest. Fourteen girls aged between 18 and 26. "Most are not older than 20 or 21," Mr Caldera remarks in a peculiar, reassuring tone.

Dr Sri Lal Caldera is a doctor of sociology. There are a lot of colourful rumours about him locally. A rumour has been circulating in Colombo that Dr Caldera (50) married last year's winner. Before the contest, I tackle him gently about this on the terrace at the GFH. No, this is not true. He is, in fact, married, presumably happily, with a daughter of 19 and son 16. "I just went to Japan with last year's winner – to the Asia Pacific Cultural Queen Finals, in Tokyo . . . but I did have an affair with the winner of the contest in 1999," he admits disarmingly.

Does his wife know all about this? No. Can I write about it? Oh yes, it's over now.

Mr Caldera introduces me to his friends as "the man from the BBC". I've had this problem before . . . in these parts the BBC is synonymous with British journalism, photography, TV and radio. They'll probably be delighted to hear that back at Bush House. If you're from the British media, you are from the BBC. The Department of Immigration even stamped my residency visa 'BBC Correspondent' despite my accreditation and letters from *The Daily Telegraph*. When I told Frances Harrison, the local BBC correspondent, she explained. "They've run out of cardboard files so they put everybody in the BBC file." This bureaucratic infelicity will later bring me serious trouble . . .

Mr Caldera explains this is not your usual beauty contest. "This is cultural." Oh, good. The girls are judged on five parameters. They get up to 20 marks for their hair; twenty for their teeth; twenty for their skin. Then apparently they get twenty marks for . . .. Mr Caldera flexes his arm and taps his muscle. For their muscles? No. Physique, apparently. The last category I don't quite understand. This is 'age' in terms of its relation to the other factors. This is a difficult concept for me to cope with. Maybe it's cultural. A taxi driver is rather more explicit in his explanation. Their hair should be like silk. Their teeth should have the glitter of sapphires. Their hips be like water jugs and their skin the colour of gold . . . Apparently, before pitching up they have all passed intelligence and 'photogenic' tests. The photographer covering the event later tells me they've also provided medical certificates attesting to their unsullied state.

Mr Caldera keeps emphasising. "These are poor girls." By way of explanation, "This is a big privilege, an opportunity for these village girls. Colombo people get everything, all the privileges, all the opportunities. They organise all the beauty contests. The contestants all speak English, the girls wear swimsuits. These are poor girls, they come here in their village costume. Most of these girls are staying here in a hotel for the first time. These are poor girls." Mr Caldera is evidently a man with a big heart. This is apparently their big opportunity. Fourteen of them are staying together in Room 181 just across the corridor from me. I know because they are gathered in the corridor, waiting for somebody to pitch up with the key. Some are practising their catwalk appearance but most are simply jabbering away excitedly.

The rewards are certainly there for them. A deal with the government-owned insurance company has secured an insurance policy worth SLR 100,000 (around $1200) for all the losers; 500,000 for the winner and 300,000 and 200,000 respectively for second and third contestants. That's big money around here and the policy is payable in twenty years time . . .

The judges are your normal sort of judges. A famous actress, Getha Kumarasinghe; a magazine editor, a chap from the Ministry of Media and Mass Communications, and so on. I ask Mr Caldera if he has any tips as to who might win. Pointing over at an adjacent table, Caldera picks out a slightly chubby, homely looking girl. He indicates that she is 'likely' to win.

The contest starts a good two hours late. Apparently, we've been waiting for promised government ministers who've failed to pitch up. That's not much of a surprise. The girls are charming, graceful and some are stunning. It seems to me Miss Chubby Chops will have some competition.

It's your usual sort of contest. Catwalk stuff. Dancers while the judges make up their minds. Shortlist. Interviews and a required attempt to sing a song. All under the searching examination of the television cameras. A good two and a half hours.

And the winner is . . . well, you know who. I speak to some of the judges after the show. They seem a little perplexed by the final result. The actress, clearly a woman of the world, simply observes with a shrug of her shoulders, "Well, Caldera counted the votes."

The lucky winner departed that night on the bus to her village near Minneriya, far away on the eastern side of the island. The contest over, her moment of glory was in the past, all that remained was the seven hour bus ride.

Of course, though, she still had May to look forward to. The Asia Pacific Championships in the company of Mr Caldera . . .

Anyway, other circumstances would intercede.

Mr Caldera would be safely hospitalised with a dicky ticker.

Entertained by the LTTE

I have been visiting other hotels elsewhere on the island during January 2002 and I am teasing Mr Lalith Rodrigo on the veranda. He has been the managing director at the GFH for some thirty years: he says he can't actually remember when he arrived. He hasn't quite built up the longevity of Kuttan – or, indeed, my trishaw driver who has been working off the front of the hotel for 47 years – but he is full of the most entertaining stories. Qualified as a lawyer, his business card announces J Lalith Rodrigo M.A. Oxon. Bar-at-Law, *ennui* with the world of law set in. "I came here to advise on legal matters, and so on, and just stayed . . ."

He is an urbane sort of chap who remains seemingly unflappable in the most trying of circumstances. And there are plenty of those in a place like the GFH.

I have been up staying as a guest of the Liberation Tigers of Tamil Eelam – or LTTE to use rather less of a mouthful – in the so-called 'uncleared areas', i.e. rebel-held areas where the government forces are unable to penetrate. Mr Rodrigo, always interested in potential competition, is interested in the hotel in which I have been staying in the jungles of the remote Vanni region.

The unpronounceable Paraiyanalankulam is where the Tiger territory of the Vanni began in those days. It is eight hours by train north of Colombo – and then a further hour or so by bus or car from the northern frontier town of Vavuniya. From 1999 up until early 2002, it was the only official crossover point for goods and transport into those parts of northern Sri Lanka known as the Vanni and held by the LTTE.

A narrow strip of red-dirt road leaves the main metalled 'highway' between Vavuniya and Mannar. On either side are abandoned rice paddies and stray cattle. After the Sri Lanka army security and search areas you enter a No Man's Land managed by the International Committee of the Red Cross.

Delegates of the ICRC from half a dozen countries, with their white coverall tops emblazoned with red crosses and clutching crackling walkie-talkies, clear the passage of trucks and people from one side to the other. Without their presence between the warring parties this crossover point would never ever have existed. Even the trucks in convoy waiting to cross and trans-ship goods have the flag of the Red Cross stretched tightly over the roofs.

People entering government territory come virtually empty-handed, without luggage or parcels. They wait patiently in the baking sun in long lines: some days as many as 600 people will pass over, not including young children. Upon their return they are fully laden: literally groaning under the weight of sacks full of goods unavailable in the Vanni. There are bicycles, medicines, baby milk, plastic chairs, spare wheels, spare inner tubes, spare anything that is unavailable to the north. An organised porterage system facilitates the movement of thousands of packages and parcels. The porters who move these new acquisitions across the lines can make up to seven or eight thousand rupees a day (up to US$100).

Lt. Milton Tissera of the Sri Lanka army (SLA) is in day to day charge of the checkpoint. He is a sympathetic man. "These are poor people," he reflects. "When I see them with their new bicycles I know just how they feel. I came from a poor family and when I was a boy the thing I most wanted in the world was a bicycle. One day I heard of someone selling a bicycle for thirty rupees – that was a lot of money in 1956. It took me six months to work and save for that bicycle. I put ten rupees down after two months and eventually the fellow let me have it for just twenty-five. But every day I would go by and stroke that bicycle imagining it to be mine. So I understand how these people feel."

In fact, it was previously not permitted to import bicycles into LTTE territory at all. On the first day that controls were relaxed, January 15 2002, 500 were imported. Within days, the gleaming new velocipedes had arrived in the remotest villages, objects of wonder and envy. Today a new bicycle – on the government side of the lines – costs around five thousand rupees. When it gets to the other side its import is taxed, at almost 50%, and together with transport it will cost around eight thousand rupees in Tiger land. Almost a hundred dollars.

Once past a white flag fluttering from a post at the side of the road you are in the putative state of Tamil Eelam: an unrecognised, impoverished land untouched by nearly all the things accepted as normal, even in most of the Third World. There is no television; no running water; no drainage; no electricity. The road system, such as it is, is a shambolic disaster after nineteen years of war and neglect.

***

When the war for Tamil Eelam really kicked off in July 1983, these were metalled roads. Now they are but cratered and potholed dirt tracks, the tarmacadam broken up and washed away long ago by years of tropical rains. The trees of the secondary jungle press close to the road. Passage is slow and arduous. Bone-shaking might sound hackneyed as a description but it is as good a way to describe it as any. There are virtually no cars: a few aged and battered trucks and a few buses constitute most of the motorised traffic. The bicycle is the mode of transport for most people. The really smart and privileged travel by motor bike. Then there are the Austin Cambridges and Morris Oxfords, with a smattering of A40s, and the odd Riley or Morris Minor.

In January, the LTTE decides to put on a rare show for the media. We are to be permitted to enter Tiger territory. The other journalists arrive in their four-wheel drives, vans and regular transport. I have walked to the 'border' crossing point having arrived by train and then bus. This provides me with the opportunity for an interesting journey.

My mode of travel is a magnificent two-tone lime and grey Austin Cambridge. I guess it dates from 1958 or 1959. I sit in the back between two senior LTTE cadres from the political wing. I've met many displaced people in my travels but here is a novelty. I am told this is a 'displaced' motor car: it was formerly in use in Jaffna before the Sri Lankan army retook the city in December 1995. From there it was evacuated to Kilinochchi, now the centre of LTTE administration, and today its driver ferries the gentlemen of the Political Wing around the dirt tracks of Tamil Eelam. It is clearly, for him, an object of great pride and has been meticulously cleaned and polished. There may be the odd piece of rust showing through but the overall impression is of a cherished conveyance. Extras abound. A bunch of plastic grapes swings jauntily from the interior mirror; a plastic fan perches on the dashboard; a poppy air freshener does its work and, on the back shelf, are matching plastic swans providing elegant cradles for vividly coloured plastic flowers. This really is motoring as it should be . . .

The car runs on kerosene and either vegetable or coconut oil keeps the moving parts of the engine going smoothly. Spares are impossible to find so resourceful wayside mechanics knock up spare parts in their workshops. The driver tells me that the springs fail rather regularly, which is hardly surprising. Although the front of the car bears two matching metal English AA badges from the 1960s, the Automobile Association could hardly be relied upon around here. The suspension is rather harder than your average British middle class family would have found comfortable for their Sunday afternoon run back in the 1950s, but the ride is actually remarkably comfortable given the state of the roads. On the way back I will be obliged to travel in CNN's Toyota van (the Cambridge will be undergoing one of those wayside repairs) and the ride will not compare at all favourably with the aged Austin, despite my being firmly sandwiched between Mr Thaya Master and Mr Sudha.

They are both from the Political Wing of the LTTE. Mr Master (so called, rather logically, because he used to be a teacher) is an engaging humorous fellow who laughs a lot and makes light of everything. Well, almost everything. He tells me he met British journalist Marie Colvin from *The Sunday Times* the previous year. When I ask him about her return journey, across the lines at night, on which she came under fire and lost an eye to a piece of Sri Lankan army shrapnel, all I get is a terse, "No comment, please." It is almost seven years since journalists have *officially* penetrated the heartland of the Liberation Tigers of Tamil Eelam. The *Sunday Times* journalist did make it in last year, but got herself blown up on the way out. But on January 15 the Tigers' lair was opened up to a pack of journalists *en masse* . . .

I leave it a couple of hours before I mention Dhanu, the LTTE suicide bomber who did for former Indian Prime Minister Rajiv Gandhi. I ask why she is not accorded martyr status. "No comment, please." I try not to pile on the difficult questions but as we pass a school packed with smartly dressed kids in blue shorts and white pleated dresses I cannot resist asking a question about the forcible recruitment of children into the LTTE. Apparently, this never takes place. The abduction of children is by "criminal elements". Yes, there is crime in Tamil Eelam: there is also a police force, court system and there are prisons.

Mr Sudha on the other side is a man of fewer words. He says he is from the political wing. I think he understands rather more English than he pretends. He is senior to Mr Master and is clearly The Boss. The only real entertainment I get out of him is when he fishes inside his shirt and produces a cyanide capsule which hangs around his neck at all times in case of capture; he also wears a tinplate metal tag stamped LTTE with his personal identification number. It's only the following evening that I notice he has about his person a modern 9mm pistol on a black canvas belt: a mean-looking Czech-made CZ 700.

The first stop is at the Circuit Bungalow at Madhu, a sacred shrine to the local people. There have been suggestions this may become home to the forthcoming peace negotiations. It would be hard to think of anywhere more suitable. The church looks magnificent in its painted blue and cream livery, the legend AVE MARIA painted in large letters across the façade. It is now fully restored after its October 1999 tank shelling in a Sri Lanka army offensive. Locals say 43 people were killed around the church. Today, Madhu has attracted almost 4,000 displaced families who live in humble shacks around the church, their daily needs cared for by the UNHCR. Says Mr S Jagenathan, local Sri Lanka Red Cross chairman, "We pray to God to bring peace here at Mahdu shrine." Around 25% of the local inhabitants are Christians; but Hindus also come to worship at the shrine. Mr Jagenathan says he does not have a political agenda. "We want our rights. That is all. We just want to be treated as equals. We are all Sri Lankans."

At a nothing place called Palamudi, a couple of hours or so north from Madhu, three roads meet. Here people change vehicles, drivers rest, rapid repairs are undertaken by wayside mechanics. One man sits in a shack at a Singer sewing machine. There are a couple of large notice boards bearing warning of the danger of mines. One is particularly direct in its artistic approach depicting a man in the process of having his leg blown off. There is little in the way of permanent structures by the side of the road: just a few shacks of wood or mud with roofs of dried coconut palm. The only constructions of any scale or permanence are the Martyrs' graveyards packed with neatly painted tombs and which are surrounded by white-painted walls boasting metal gates. Clearly no effort, or expense, is spared in their maintenance.

In the so-called 'uncleared areas' – those under the control of the LTTE – there is total darkness once night falls around seven in the evening. There is no electricity supply – no water supply either, for that matter - and the black of night is pierced just occasionally by an oil lamp at a roadside shack, a bicycle repair centre or an arrack bar selling the locally brewed version of the spirit distilled from the juice of the coconut, so popular throughout the island. In the darkness, people are putting up bunting and flags. Tomorrow is January 16 and is the day on which the LTTE celebrate the martyrdom of Kittu, a leader who died in 1993. Intercepted by the Indian Navy, he blew up the ammunition ship he was travelling aboard at the entrance to Madras Harbour. The LTTE are strong on remembering their martyrs.

Eight uncomfortable hours from the crossover point and we come to the town of Mallavi. To say Mallavi comes as a surprise is something of an understatement. After hours of travelling in darkness, it appears as an oasis of light. Here there are evidently ample means to cast light in dark places.

The Mallavi Hotel is a sort of legend. I actually thought it was an urban myth. Someone in Colombo once told me that the LTTE operated a luxury hotel in the heart of their jungle territory but I dismissed it as some sort of arrack-borne fantasy. In fact, the dinner party tale turns out to be an understatement, if anything. Set in its own well-lit compound, amidst meticulously tended gardens, the hotel boasts power, water and mosquito nets, draped around *bijou* miniature four-poster beds. At the front entrance to the long, low bungalow are two rubber mats bearing the legend, in English, WELCOME. Despite our late arrival, we are seated to a positive banquet of fresh seafood and cooked meats served by white-gloved waiters.

The *piece de resistance* has to be the conference room with its hardwood furniture, polished wooden floor and walls and 240 volt air conditioning. The table of the conference room is adorned with a miniature tiger flag on a pedestal: a full toothed tiger in yellow set over crossed assault rifles and yellow sun all set on a revolutionary red background. The whole is presided over by an almost life size framed photograph of Velupillai Prabhakaran: the photograph fails to disguise his modest stature and a pronounced middle age spread. He no longer has the moustache he used to sport – people say it started to show grey hairs and he had it removed. He looks more favourite uncle than a dedicated genius in the war and terror department.

With dawn the Mallavi Hotel and its surroundings are subject to a reverent closer examination by its guests. The heavy padlock on the gate is undone. It bears the *imprimateur* SHANGHAI CHINA H 406. Throughout the garden are flowers, rose bushes and plants in neatly tended beds, their borders marked by painted 122mm. artillery shell casings. Those containing plants are interspersed with upturned, white painted casings. Then there are dotted here and there cupola awnings affording shade to plastic tables and chairs. This is where high level meetings take place; where foreigners come to meet the leadership of the LTTE. As we sit sheltered by the sun under the protective awnings, waiters in black tie and wearing white gloves serve glasses of cool lemonade.

Above the door to the conference room there is a small plaque with a map of the island. Etched out in gold is the perceived future state of Tamil Eelam. Tamil Eelam appears to occupy fully two thirds of the coastline, around half of the land mass and appears to extend as far south as Negombo, just to the north of the capital, and down to Yala in the south east of the country, taking in all of the north and east, a fair bit of the west and Uva province in the centre.

We are, of course, gathered in this cosseted luxury for a serious purpose. Shortly after 10 a.m. a camouflaged Pajero sweeps into the compound. It bears the person of Mr Paramu Thamilchelvam, chief of the LTTE's political wing since 1993, flanked by a trio of bodyguards in freshly pressed Tiger camouflage uniforms. It is said he is number three in the hierarchy, after Prabhakaran and the chief of the intelligence wing: he is worth protecting. It is said that he was one of the prime targets of the Sri Lankan army's successful deep penetration team – the Long Range Reconnaissance Patrol

(LRRP) – which, until December 24 had been working behind the lines assassinating senior LTTE cadres. The success of the LRRP had become of extreme concern to the LTTE but the whole operation was compromised on January 2 when the safe house of the team at Athurigiriya, just outside Colombo, was raided by police in an apparently unauthorised operation. Weapons, including Tiger uniforms, were seized and five of the undercover agents were arrested and their operations compromised as a result of rivalries and lack of cooperation within the Sri Lankan security services. Responsible for the death of the cadre Shankar – formerly one of Prabhakaran's right hand men – the team developed a capability for working and remaining behind the lines in LTTE territory. Thamilchelvam himself only narrowly escaped their attentions in a claymore mine attack.

Thamilchelvam is not what you might expect. He is bespectacled, slight in build and with an apparently sunny disposition. He beams most of the time. He is either very pleased with himself indeed, or an excellent showman. Probably the latter. A Colombo newspaper terms him 'the notorious terrorist masquerading as a politician'. His press conference is packed and lasts almost two hours. My understanding is that he understands English but prefers to fence the questions in Tamil through the medium of an elderly and expert interpreter.

He uses a two hour question and answer session to make a series of politically inspired points. Most importantly, he makes it clear that peace talks will not take place unless the LTTE is de-proscribed by the government in Colombo. "The ban on the LTTE has to be lifted then only will we be equal partners in the talks. A lifting of the ban is a must because it is not prudent for us to talk as an illegitimate party."

Although he answers most questions directly, he skilfully avoids what might be regarded as the more substantive issues. Asked possibly the most key question: as to whether the LTTE would be willing to drop its demand for a separate independent state of Tamil Eelam – clearly a demand unacceptable in Colombo – he blandly observes, "We do not feel it prudent to commit ourselves on this question at this juncture."

He denies that the LTTE had evinced a desire for peace in the wake of September 11 and the worldwide assault on terrorism. "We were shocked when many countries put us on the terrorist list ... we believe there is no substantial case for that. That happened largely because of propaganda and misinformation against us and the successful lobbying by the Sri Lankan government in the corridors of world power. We are confident that one day we will be accepted as a liberation organisation fighting against a rogue state which practises state terrorism. I must assure you that September 11 had little to do with our decision to go for talks. We had expressed our desire for talks long before the September 11 attacks ..."

***

A comment on the peace process, towards the very end of the session, served to emphasise a considerable degree of reserve. "We would like to repeat - over and over again – that this is just a preliminary stage."

It would seem evident that the LTTE strategy now involves playing a long – possibly very long – game. Members of the political wing of the LTTE talk much about the restoration of the civil and political rights of Tamils in Sri Lanka and. Says Thamilchelvam, "The new government [in Colombo] should attend to the needs of the people as experienced here. Time is an essential factor. [Only] changes will lay the *foundations* for peace negotiations ..." Talks about talks, facilitated by representatives of the Norwegian government will likely extend over a very considerable period of time. Thamilchelvam sees the Norwegians acting as facilitators; once substantive talks might start "we could perhaps have a mediator".

To a degree, an extended period of preparations for talks which, may or may not take place, will suit the government in Colombo as it seeks to draw breath after its December 5 election victory; and seeks to draw away pressure from bodies like the IMF and the World Bank. Although it will not be possible to significantly reduce security measures or the scale of the armed forces, except at serious risk to the future survival of the Sri Lankan state as an undivided entity, the absence of a shooting war on the ground will at least enable a halt in expensive weapons purchases.

However, a lengthy interregnum of peace will be of immeasurable benefit to the LTTE. It is clear that the whole administrative structure in LTTE territory is vulnerable after 19 years of war; it requires to recruit large numbers of cadres; restock with arms and munitions; repair infrastructure; and to kick start its own very basic economy with the largely unrestricted imports allowed under the ceasefire agreement with Colombo. Thamilchelvam himself admits, "Our infrastructure is completely devastated by war. . . the new government [in Colombo] should bring normalcy. The economic embargo should be lifted in total." A total lifting of the embargo would allow in, amongst other dual technology items, cement, batteries and barbed/razor wire, presently specifically banned. There is already anecdotal evidence of instructions from headquarters in Kilinochchi for traders to stock up well on previously banned items. Six or twelve months of peace would be of enormous strategic benefit, I remember reflecting at the time.

There is no doubt that the nascent state of Tamil Eelam remains firmly a one party state based around a cult of personality in turn centred upon its charismatic leader Velupillai Prabhakaran. The movement's political philosophy seems undiluted: Thamilchelvam repeatedly used the phrase 'Sinhala masses' indicative of an anachronistic political philosophy which might be regarded as quaint if it were not so menacing.

Despite the undoubted hardships endured by those living under LTTE rule there is no evidence whatsoever of any diminution in popular support; rather to the contrary. In that respect the LTTE remains a formidable enemy which has thus far managed to retain the initiative in the peace process. It will likely retain that initiative.

The trip provides much good copy and I write it up for both *The Daily Telegraph* and for *Janes Intelligence Review*. The *Telegraph* article gives me some scope for dwelling on the delightful eccentricities of our stay and of our transport. The article is, of course, picked up by the LTTE. When I meet Mr Master a few weeks later he is not quite as cheerful as last time. "Very interesting article, Mr Harris. Much about Austin Cambridge but very little about the suffering of Tamil people." A perceptive fellow. A black mark against me, I fear.

***

Lalith listens intently to my tale of the LTTE's generous hospitality in the Vanni. He clearly picks up on the most important point from the perspective of the seasoned hotelier. "I can see we've got to get our chaps into wearing white gloves if we're going to compete in the future," he observes drily.

Excellent though the Mallavi Hotel was, I can't say it is my favourite in the Sri Lankan firmament. The one I'm thinking about, as I wrote this in 1997, might then have been the nearest thing to paradise . . .

The turquoise blue waters of the Indian Ocean ripple gently onto pure white, palm-fringed sands which stretch away to infinity. My cool, air-conditioned hotel room opens directly onto the beach and, of a morning, it is an effortless 100 yard sprint into the clear, warm waters of the ocean. For the snorkeler, just beyond the gentle surf there are stunning, white coral reefs and shoals of exotic tropical fish. A couple of miles offshore over the water lies Pigeon Island, breeding ground for the Blue Rock Pigeon. It is said Admiral Lord Nelson used the island for gunnery practice.

Over a breakfast of fresh pineapple it is already time to consider dinner. Yes, lobster, would be fine and a boatman is engaged to catch your dinner. Here, there's no pollution, no sewage. No hawkers on the beach - well, there is one inoffensive chap on a bicycle selling spectacular conches at fifty pence a go. No deafening disco. No drunken louts. No noise of jet skis. No film of suntan oil on the clear, still waters of the swimming pool. As the sun sets over the Indian Ocean and the blue sea turns a reddish grey you tuck into curry, rice and perfectly prepared lobster, sweeter and fleshier than it seemed possible to imagine.

Members of staff busy themselves catering for your every need. This all sounds so perfect that you might rightly wonder when I tell you I am sometimes the only guest in the Nilaveli Beach Hotel. That, indeed, there are frequently no guests at all despite the derisory fifteen dollars a night price tag. It should be at the top of the list of Asia's dream hotels. But Nilaveli (pronounced Nee-laa - vely) is the last remaining, fully functioning luxury hotel on the whole of the east coast of troubled Sri Lanka.

Manager Mr V Prem Kumar says that, most of the time, he just sits in the hotel alone with 20 members of staff. For the 26 year-old Nilaveli Beach Hotel is right on the front line in Sri Lanka's long running war: it effectively exists as an oasis of luxury and safety in a no man's land. It is, indeed, a strange, bizarre haven and its continued existence is something of a mystery even to those who are in on the secret.

In the early 1980s, tourist hotels mushroomed along the north east coast of Sri Lanka near the port of Trincomalee, or 'Trinco' as it is known, dubbed 'the best natural harbour in the world' by Nelson. The vast white beaches and the warm, blue waters combined with mean temperatures around 28 degrees made it perfect for tourist development. The science fiction writer Arthur C Clarke, from his base in the Sri Lankan capital of Colombo, bought land for a deep sea diving school and investors poured into the area.

But a bloody attack on the Sri Lankan army in July 1983 announced the emergence in the north of the country of a radical, Marxist-style leader, Velupillai Prabhakaran. A ruthless ideologue, he sought to lead the minority Tamil population, concentrated in the north and east of Sri Lanka, into an independent state of Tamil Eelam. Soon Sri Lanka was plunged into ethnic conflict as majority Sinhalese fought Tamils in the streets of the cities, including Trinco. Up until the summer of 1985, the hotels on the east coast were full with western tourists but, that year, the tentacles of war spread here.

Most of the Colombo-based owners abandoned their hotels to looting and decay: just next door the Blue Lagoon hotel lies deserted and ruined. In 1985, the Moonlight Hotel, just a couple of hundred metres the other side of the Nilaveli Beach Hotel, was blown up by the Tamil fighters. Its eerie, collapsed ruins and its stagnant, sludge filled swimming pool stand in silent testimony to what happens to a tourist industry when war arrives.

Somehow Nilaveli stubbornly remained in business - with virtually no business to speak of - as the war ranges around it. The military checkpoints - sixteen of them in total - start 70 miles back down the road towards Colombo. The barman reminisces about the summer of 1985 when there were almost three hundred guests packed into the 90 rooms laid out in whitewashed, terraced bungalows. Empty it may be today, but it is not operated as some sort of cheap, gimcrack joint: towels are changed twice a day, there are fresh sheets on the bed daily.

A photograph of a throng of extravagantly uniformed and sarong-clad staff at the opening in 1974 hanging in the office demonstrates that things are not quite as they were. Nevertheless, as the tropical dawn breaks at 7 a.m., a dozen or so workers are already busying themselves scooping overnight fallen leaves from the pool, brushing the tennis court, polishing the tiled floor of the open-sided restaurant, sandpapering and varnishing its columns of coconut timber, sweeping the paths which wind through the low fruit and beech trees connecting the bungalows to the main block. They are even sweeping the beach to smooth the sand for the day's single visitor. Royalty could hardly fare better.

These days, there's usually just the odd journalist or aid worker while Mr Kumar patiently waits for the tourists to come back. But Sri Lanka's war shows no sign of ending with devastating bomb attacks in the cities, guerilla war in the countryside, naval attacks by the Sea Tigers on ports like Trinco, and assassinations of military and political figures by 'Black Tiger' suicide bombers. Against this background, as you make your way up the narrow, broken road to Nilaveli, through rigorous army checkpoints looking for batteries (the Tigers need these for their suicide bomb kits), and through the heavy iron gates set in a high wall, the place is a bit of an enigma.

Mr Kumar is, first and foremost, a professional hotelier who professes to enjoy his work. He also seems to be a bit of a philosopher which must be something of a prerequisite in his position. Born in Jaffna, in the Tamil heartland in the north of the country, he's married to a Christian. "Same roof, different houses but the roof always safeguards you when it rains." He believes that men should live in peace. That in this limited time on earth we should behave to each other as brothers. That it is the politicians who cause problems in the pursuit of power.

Yes, but how does this hotel survive when all around are destroyed; in an area where the military abandon any attempt to control the roads after nightfall and the LTTE control supreme; where residents of the nearby Moslem village of Iqbal Nagar fled their homes two years ago, when the LTTE attacked the police post ? They elected to take everything with them, including roofs and window frames, never to return.

"Well, you see, this hotel is running in a neutral way. We are not interested in politics. We just do hotel business." The owners have other interests in hotels and tourism but business must surely be at an all time low? Mr Kumar shrugs his shoulders, "We have a few guests. We survive." The reflection of the floodlights and fairylights twinkle in the waters of the pool ($300 a month to maintain) and, just beyond, arc lights illuminate the entire beach frontage for hundreds of yards in both directions. At dawn and dusk, flak-jacketed army patrols, machine guns at the ready, fan out across the beach. They are retreating to the safety of their fortified bases during the hours of darkness.

Says one of Sri Lank'a most resilient hoteliers as the deep boom of shellfire penetrates the night, "It is a very long way away, maybe fifty miles. Don't worry." Sound travels far in the still of the tropical night. And he adds, in some sort of eastern continuance of the tradition of the Windmill Theatre, "We will never give up. We will never lose hope. We will never close."

People in faraway Colombo - to them this is an impenetrable war zone - have their own theories. The assistant to a government minister told me, "They pay off the Tigers *and* they keep the army sweet." Mr Kumar vehemently denies this but, nevertheless, the war goes on all around, rarely touching the calm of Nilaveli. "The LTTE may go to the villages but they do not come here. The management at the Midnight Hotel made a big mistake - they took sides." In fact, I am told they simply asked the local police to guard the hotel - around here that was quite enough to constitute taking sides. Last January, the LTTE did scale the high walls around the hotel and attack the buildings. The staff say they were just hungry: they gave them food and they went away.

An English expatriate in Colombo who visited the hotel from time to time has some rather more hair-raising accounts. "Last year, the Tigers came up the beach in rubber boats firing AK-47s. The fire-fight went on for two hours as we took cover in our rooms . . .". One memorable Sunday, more than 100 Sri Lanka army officers and their wives were busily engaged in drinking the hotel dry by the pool (they don't pay for their drinks, apparently), when the Tigers arrived all tooled up. There was an uneasy standoff. The military pulled out . . . the Tigers took their seats by the pool and started up where their enemies had left just left off.

It was rather quieter last weekend. We talk on the terrace as the sun slips down, and there is that long, deep rumbling sound. Mr Kumar looks pained. I forebore to comment.

By April of 2002, within weeks of the accord signed between the UNP government and the LTTE, the Nilaveli Beach Hotel had become quite the most fashionable place to stay on the whole island. For weeks, at fashionable Colombo dinner parties, guests would regale each other with tales of their visit to the newly accessible hotel and the beaches of the east. Getting a room was virtually impossible and when I visited that month whilst on a trip to the east, the beach was crowded with thousands of weekend holidaymakers. A squad of unformed security men tried vainly to drive the incursors off hotel property, where they occupied seats and spread out their picnics, blithely insouciant of the economics of the hotel trade. The peace which, ironically, had accompanied war was quite gone and the whole experience had degenerated into the most noisy and frightful vulgarity. I never returned

***

End of February and I espy a tall, gangling figure lurking locally in the entrance hall of the GFH. His slim, almost emaciated, frame is bestrewn with three dangling Leica M6s. The hallmark of a real photographer. The mop of silver hair, the lived-in, lined face suggests a certain distinction and I am intrigued. I introduce myself and discover the legendary Tim Page, doyenne of war photographers.

Page is staying in the hotel as he plans several island-wide trips in search of images for a new book on Sri Lanka. We sit on the terrace as the sun sinks into the sea. A group of local photographers are energetically and enthusiastically photographing a couple of female models. One is dusky skinned and sexy with a sarong wrapped over a pair of tight shorts. The other sports a red top and figure hugging black lycra micro-miniskirt below a bare midriff. They lounge and spread themselves for the photographers, evidently a workshop on portraiture. They are earnest and eager and snap the girls from every possible angle. Surveying the scene, Page observes drily, "What's all this tripod stuff. Can't they hold a camera steady?"

Maybe they're too excited, I suggest.

***

It is not quite April Fool's Day. It is Sunday March 31st to be precise. But I look at the flyer on the table on the verandah in disbelief. The 138 year-old Galle Face Hotel is offering donkey rides. Perish the thought. Meantime, over my shoulder, a trio of Sri Lankans, dressed as Mexicans complete with straw sombreros, are tuning their guitars. The strains of *Guantanamera* pierce the air, drowning out the sound of the sea, as the purveyors of calypso and Latin culture serenade unfortunate couples at their bargain buffet lunch.

New management is in place at the hotel. Mr Anura Lokuhetty, battle hardened veteran of numerous sunshine holiday hotels in the south of the island, has arrived in the august halls of the GFH. He is not impressed by what he has found. Sanjeev has decided to attempt to modernize the hotel and renovate the long abandoned south wing, closed up by his father in the early 1970s. This does not augur well, in my view.

***

June and the south west monsoon has arrived. It has been presaged in the third week of May by heavy rain early evening most days. This is particularly disagreeable because it debars me from enjoying the sunset, gin and tonic in hand, from my balcony.

The onset of monsoon seems to coincide with the festival of Vesak. I don't like these long holidays, anyway. Everybody is away and businesses are closed for up to a week. The hotel has closed the bar and alcohol is not available with meals for a full week. This seems an odd way to celebrate but I defer uncomplainingly to local customs. A few years ago, when the old retainers on the staff were in control, they would serve me beer in a teapot with my curry and rice. This I would religiously pour into a china cup bearing the shield logos of the GFH. Alas, new management and a psychosis of fear instilled into the staff has put an end to this valued concession.

What with no drinks, no rich red sunsets and few visitors, the GFH is now a distinctly gloomy place and I resolve not to be around in future at this time of year. Some days, the normally azure blue sea alternates between muddy green and grey, with angry, foamy breakers rolling ashore. It's more like the cold North Sea than the Indian Ocean. Sudden wind announces the imminent arrival of rain, which sets the waiters scurrying to remove tablecloths from the plastic tables in the open air. Nobody sits at them anyway: I wonder why they bother. Some days the wind has been particularly strong. The other afternoon it completely took away the corrugated metal canopy above the balcony off the office in my suite. It was carried away like some oversized Frisbee landing on a flight of steps below. I hesitate to think what would have happened if some unfortunate bather had been *en route* to the pool. I suppose they could well have been decapitated. A few days later, the much larger canopy off my bedroom is lifted from its supports by the wind and peeled back so that it tilts down crazily. Symptoms of the physical decay of the edifice of the GFH seem to be rather in evidence.

At five o'clock this morning cyclonic gusts of wind seem to have noisily removed a considerable part of the roof. For some ten minutes, the crashing and clattering of debris bouncing off the canopies on the way down is deafening. By daylight, the balcony is piled with shattered asbestos. Asbestos doesn't have a high reputation as a building material in Europe and America these days. Well, staff and guests don't seem to be expiring so I suppose it must be OK.

But the monsoon winds presage a draughty future for yours truly.

'Rumour not humour'

In May I made a speech to Colombo North Rotary Club, up the road from the GFH at the Ceylon Continental Hotel. I'd been at a reception thrown by the Belgian Consul in the ballroom of the GFH and met a Rotarian who was intrigued to establish I shared the same name as the founder of Rotary. I was promptly invited to speak: I'm rather used to this. It's happened all over the world. I'm usually invited on the basis of nomenclature rather than anything else.

Anyway, I had made several trips to the east of the country and was genuinely amazed at what was happening under the guise of the peace process. I revealed what I had found out during my travels. The audience appeared genuinely amazed, rather to my own astonishment. It was as clear as daylight, I thought, what was going on. But I guess I rather misjudged the local reaction. Simultaneously, a 3,000 word edition of my analysis appeared in London in *Jane's Intelligence Review*.

Shortly afterwards, I had a bit of a run-in one Saturday evening with the Prime Minister across the road at the Galadari Hotel. It was a private party, in a room off the lobby, packed with UNP stalwarts like Nimal Cooke of the Maharaja Organisation, Desmond Fernando and the editor of *The Sunday Leader*, Lasantha Wickremetunge. The party was thrown by Nirj Deva. Nirj is a Sri Lankan made good on the world stage: once an adviser to no less than Iron Lady Margaret Thatcher and latterly a Member of the European Parliament and 'Special Advisor' to the British Conservative Party. It emerges that Ranil, who is three hours late arriving and finally pitches up at 11.15, has just appointed Nirj his 'Ambassador at Large' in Europe. Nirj is an amiable sort of cove. Very good at saying the right thing, with actually getting his tongue too firmly locked in important orifices.

Nirj sportingly attempts to introduce me to the PM. My proffered hand is ignored and Ranil observes pithily, "I know perfectly well who you are and I have only one thing to say to you. I am not the man who is going to give Sri Lanka away."

Ranil is soon blowing off about the UNP's achievements and grand ambitions. Some of this stuff is really quite entertaining albeit alternately drawn from Peter Pan and Hans Christian Anderson. When he announces that Trincomalee is to be the site of Sri Lanka's Formula One racetrack I fear I cannot keep silent any longer.

"Do you have the permission of the LTTE for that?" I venture to ask. There is an unpleasant silence until one of the party faithful reassures the PM. "Don't pay any attention to that monkey." I decide that discretion is now the better part of valour, thank Nirj and leave the room.

The following Monday, the police arrived at the Galle Face Hotel and quizzed Mr Perera, the manager, and prevailed on him to supply information about my movements and general activities. Within a week, my suite would be searched on at least two occasions I could identify. Nothing was taken but the 007 agents assigned to the task must have got thirsty. They took a can of coke from the fridge, drank it and tossed the empty can in the waste basket. And a poor chap would take up position underneath a coconut tree across the road from the hotel for almost two months. I started using the back entrance of the hotel which did not appear to merit surveillance.

But the first inkling that things were about to go badly wrong was eight days before my visa to work as a journalist was due to expire in November. My work as Colombo correspondent of *The Daily Telegraph* had not been exactly over-demanding as war raged in Afghanistan. The Bush coalition's liberation efforts dominated the foreign pages. But my few contributions to the *Telegraph*, and to *Janes Intelligence Review*, for which I had worked for almost ten years as an analyst on 'global insurgency and terrorism' (their words) had not gone unnoticed in the corridors of power.

In July I moved just fifty yards from the hotel into Galle

Face Court, a magnificent 1920s building. I still had a view of the Indian Ocean and the broad sweep of Galle Face Green. But, in the third week of October, I noted from my office window, as I went to bed, two men in dark trousers and white shirts. Dark trousers and loose white shirts – with the bulge of a pistol worn on the belt – are the garb characteristic of various political security divisions who appear to operate untrammelled around the Sri Lankan capital.

I had become accustomed to surveillance in Colombo. A bespectacled chap had been lounging against the wall across the road for weeks simply jangling his car keys and, before him, for more than a month there had been a chap who was dropped by van every morning and spent the daylight hours propped up in the shade of a coconut tree across the busy roundabout. Interesting job, I don't think.

My fascination with the country had been reflected in 2001 in a book of my photographs and essays *Fractured Paradise*, which was published in Colombo by Vijitha Yapa, bookseller, publisher and former newspaper editor. After the book launch at the Galle Face Hotel, addressed by the present Prime Minister's secretary, Mr Bradman Weerakoon, I was taken to dinner by the chairman of the English language crusading newspaper *The Sunday Leader*. Lal asked me if I would come and edit his paper as it looked as though the editor, his brother Lasantha, would have to leave the country by the end of the year after intimidation by the then People's Alliance (PA) government. According to Lal, over a curry dinner at the Holiday Inn Hotel, a deal had been reached. To be precise, Australian intelligence had struck a deal with the government: Lasantha would leave with his family for Australia, where they would be granted residency, and, in return, the PA strongmen would be held off. In October, though, an election was called after G L Pieris, S B Dissanyake and several other PA politicians crossed over to the opposition.

In Sri Lanka, 'crossing over' can be prompted by a range of opportunities or motives. It can, of course, be occasioned by conscience but, more likely, opportunism and incentives come into play. Amongst those who crossed over, reducing the government to a minority, were G L Pieris, a stooped, fellow of studious appearance (an Indian journalist friend, P K Balachanddran, described him eloquently as 'the coat hanger') and a veteran of such events having done it before; and S B Dissanayake, a rude, foul mouthed fellow with a brace of equally disagreeable sons. His offspring would demonstrate their startling social skills at the New Year party at the Galle Face Hotel, transforming it into a 4 a.m. shooting gallery.

During November 2001, it became increasingly clear that the electorate might opt for a change; for a new parcel of rogues. The government changed on December 5 and the job with *The Leader* evaporated as the United National Party (UNP) took over power. At the time, I didn't see that that should affect me particularly. I was remarkably content to be settled in the fading colonial splendour of the Galle Face Hotel, Colombo, as correspondent for *The Daily Telegraph* and *Jane's Intelligence Review*, writing a book and taking in a vibrant social scene. The hotel moved in some of its best antique colonial furniture into my suite. With the tourist industry then in seemingly total collapse, the management did me an excellent deal for a seafront suite overlooking the blue waters of the Indian Ocean and the gently swaying palms of the gardens. The high spot of the day for me was to sit with a gin and tonic on my balcony at the hotel watching the sun sink down into the Indian Ocean. All very agreeable for US$30 a night.

Within days of taking office, the new Prime Minister, Ranil Wickremesinghe, tangibly demonstrated that peace was in the air. Virtually all of the security barriers and checkpoints in Colombo were removed from the streets. This was, or course, universally popular. People could move about without tedious security checks and the traffic flow freed up.

This was soon followed by a ceasefire. Just before Christmas, I was at a party at the Russian Cultural Centre when the news of the ceasefire broke. The local reporter for All India Radio, Mohan Chandak, phoned me at the party.

Peace moves, brokered by the Norwegians, continued apace during January and February. A February 22 Memorandum of Agreement (thereafter referred to as the 'MOU') was, significantly, signed first by the rebel leader, Velupillai Prabhakaran, in his eyrie in the jungles of the Wanni, a full day before the Prime Minister. The President later told me she had not even seen the agreement.

There were elements of the new government's peace process which were, in my judgement, flawed and I drew attention to them. In the London *Daily Telegraph* I wrote about child conscription in the east of the country, carried out under the noses of the security forces, emasculated by the MOU with the rebels. I also wrote in *The Telegraph* of my meeting with the LTTE's eastern leader Karikalan in March He told me "it was for Tamil youth to repossess land stolen by the Muslims." This caused an uproar in Sri Lanka as soon as it was reprinted under the arrangement *The Telegraph* had with the local paper *The Island*. Another English language daily, *The Daily Mirror*, also commissioned an article from me on the meeting.

The Karikalan meeting took place during a two week long visit to the east. I had been invited to accompany an amenable and influential, if shadowy, figure who had been despatched to the east by the Prime Minister, to report on the developing situation.

Nanda Godage was an old friend who I had worked with back in 1996. A retired Sri Lankan Ambassador in Brussels and High Commissioner in New Delhi, when I first came across him he was running the Foreign Ministry for Minister Lakshman Kadrigamar. Sri Lanka had been getting a bad image in the west for its prosecution of the war. The publicity was more related to the way visiting journalists had been treated rather than conduct of the actual war and I had suggested to a friend, who turned out to be well connected, that things could be turned around by the rather simple stratagem of actually treating the press better by making modest facilities available and by a touch more transparency. I was duly taken on to write a 10,000 word report on reform of media strategy, which I completed in September 1996 after four visits that year.

I was impressed by Godage. I never actually saw him play chess but he operated like an accomplished chess player. He had an ability to see several moves ahead; to see the implications of a course of action whilst those around him were still absorbing the context of the proposal.

I visited the east with Nanda Godage and we were joined by an Indian journalist, P K Balachandran of *The Hindustan Times*. 'P.K.' was an old Sri Lanka hand who had been in the country several years. Affable and incisive as he was, I was never really sure why he actually joined us. I knew why I was there – as a sounding post, with my intelligence background, for Godage. Anyway, we made a good team and it was a revealing trip.

The visit to the east convinced me more than ever that the LTTE were up to no good. In Pottuvil (March 12) the fears of the Muslim community were clearly expressed in a series of meetings at the appropriately named Hideaway Hotel. We visited Kumari and I was moved by the plight of a woman whose son had been taken by the LTTE. Ordinary people clearly feared the stranglehold the LTTE was imposing under the guise of peace. In Ampara (March 14) I was impressed by the commitment and expertise of the local STF.

In Batticaloa, the security forces seemed under no illusion as to what was going down. What they could not understand was what Colombo was up to. On March 16 we crossed into LTTE territory in the company of the local MP, Krishnapillai. We met at his office on the border with Tiger territory. A nervous, garrulous character, the most interesting thing about the meeting was the appearance of his wife. She soon broke down into tears. She confessed the price of LTTE support for her husband's election to parliament had been their eldest son. They had handed him over to the LTTE for military training. Krishnapillai appeared unmoved by her tears and ordered up more tea.

As Nanda spoke with the Peace Secretariat and the Prime Minister's office on a Sunday morning, March 17, the sound of cannon fire broke the still of Trinco. I assumed they were practice rounds but the firing went on for a quarter of an hour or so and I could see puffs of smoke in China Bay. LTTE gunboats were probing the harbour defences.

In Muttur on March 19, the local Sinhala community revealed they had met and voted to a man, and a woman, for that matter, to leave if the security forces were to withdraw their protection.

Our trip to the east was rounded off on March 20 with an impressive briefing at military headquarters in Minneriya by Major General Sunil Tennakoon, himself a former intelligence officer. In the cool of his air conditioned office, he gave us a two hour long briefing over tea and curried sweetmeats and left us in no doubt as to his own views and, indeed, those of the military establishment generally. The LTTE were gathering men and *materiel* for war.

At Nanda's request I compiled an intelligence report for the Prime Minister drawing together all the strands of our visit and culminating in a risk assessment. This was unpaid and I did it as a favour, expecting nothing in return and thus being able to maintain my journalistic independence.

I wrote a couple of articles about the trip for the *Mirror* and my *Telegraph* articles were re-published in *The Island*.

By now, it had occurred to me that the real Achillees heel of the LTTE might be the organisation's total lack of a sense of humour. In my perception it was an unreformed and anachronistic revolutionary movement spawned a quarter of a century previously in the school of Castro and Guevera. I wrote a number of wry, mickey-taking articles. It seems that these essentially harmless, humorous articles really hit home.

The intro to one of my *Mirror* articles particularly raised the hackles of the LTTE.

These LTTE people are oh, so charming. With their cheery smiles, mild manners, warm open features and welcoming handshakes they are straight from the Saatchi & Saatchi public relations manual for Transformation of Terrorist Leaders into Genial Uncle Figures. They make the government Information Department chaps look like grumpy ogres. Who could possibly think that friendly, limping man Mr Thamil Chelvam was such a rotter? Then there's that nice man Mr Karikalan who holds court over the eastern province from his remote fastness in Kokkadicholai.

He greets you with a firm handshake, beaming genially from behind a pair of designer spectacles. He reminds you of Mole, rather than Ratty, from *Wind in the Willows*. Such a nice man . . . Somewhere in the background is that rather tasty looking girl, Banuka. I first noticed her at the Batticaloa Pongu Thamil. She gave a dynamic, powerful performance haranguing the crowd. It was infinitely more effective than that of all the politicos put together. And it was oh, so sexy. A sort of beautiful version of Margaret Thatcher. I have definitely developed a crush on her (Banuka not Margaret Thatcher). She's an absolute cracker. In more ways than one. Apparently, she sends the female cadres out into the eastern province to deal severely with male 'eve teasers'. They beckon rude boys into back streets for hoped-for hanky panky, then they beat them to pulp with karate chops. On second thoughts, I think I'll leave her alone. But I'll still have fantasies about her . . .

Welcome to Kokkadicholai. It's a nothing place. But it is the nerve centre of LTTE civil operations in the east as the HQ of political chief of the east Karikalan. That bad egg the military chief Karuna works at another location in the area known as 'Beirut'. Mr Karikalan's previous guests – a couple of dozen of them - were a group of cap-in-hand contractors from Batticaloa seeking permissions and signatures on their contracts for work in the government, cleared areas. He'a a powerful chap Mr Karikalan. Some say he's even number two to old Prabhakaran. That probably explains the slightly disturbing presence of a cadre with a loaded American M-16 assault rifle and four spare clips contained in webbing strapped to his body. I was also a bit unnerved by the fact we were being comprehensively photographed and videoed from all angles. I guess there's now my own personal LTTE file. I just hope Tamil Eelam doesn't actually encroach on Colombo. If so, I'm on the first chopper off the roof of the US Embassy.

Irreverence is, of course, well established in England as both a literary form and a political tactic. It is in its infancy in Sri Lanka and I did not then realise the truly devastating effect of humour. The day the article appeared – April 1 appropriately enough – the phone rang from early morning. Several journalist colleagues wanted to know if the rumour that I was having an affair with LTTE women's leader Banuka was true. What had been meant as wry humour became instant rumour, if not established fact.

Nanda Godage was shocked. "I hear you've dared to call Thamil Chelvan a rotter and Karuna a bad egg." He opined that there could be "very serious consequences". At the time, I found that rather amusing in itself. But I was still on the learning curve. Within days Prabhakaran had called both Karikalan and Banuka to his jungle fastness in the north for some meaningful discussions . . .

But the article which seemed to find its mark, long before it was published, thanks to some surreptitious emailing around the world, was one I wrote for *Lanka Monthly Digest*.

I'm getting a bit worried about this State of Tamil Eelam business. Don't get me wrong. I'm all in favour of small states. They encourage a bit of welcome diversity in a dull world. Small states are much more interesting than their larger neighbours. They tend to produce smashingly beautiful postage stamps, are notably emollient in the tax free trading department and are often good for getting your hands on a useful spare passport. All stuff I've been rather keen on in my peripatetic and dysfunctional existence.

So I'm watching with bated breath all this Tamil Eelam stuff. But it doesn't look too promising to me. I mean, these LTTE chaps are just so serious. I can never take anyone seriously who takes themselves seriously, if you see what I mean. I don't think the word fun is in the LTTE dictionary. I'm afraid there isn't going to be much joy for those living in the two thirds or so of the island of Sri Lanka who are going to have Velupillai Prabhakaran as their leader (President and Prime Minister rolled into one, we are advised by Chief Crony Mr Balasingham). Let me tell you about some unnerving incidents experienced whilst travelling in what is already *de facto* Tamil Eelam.

It's Pongu Tamil day in Trincomalee. A nice day for some snaps of all these colourful marchers with their bunting and their big placards of the Chief Genial Fatty. A funny thing happens as you lift your camera for a snap. A hand appears over the lens. I lower the camera and look around but can't see the origin of the hand which has left a large greasy smudge on the lens. A second attempt and the same thing happens. I look down. Below me is a diminutive Boy Scout of no more than 10 or 11 summers in pristine uniform. "No photographs," he fiercely instructs.

"Buzz off," I instruct his woggle. "Listen to me sonny, I'm a mate of your Uncle Karikalan and unless you clear off I'll report you to LTTE headquarters." This was, of course, before Karikalan fell from grace. My uniformed tormentor slopes off but eventually catches up with me. This time he has some rather larger boys with him and I decide that discretion is the better part of valour as I am marched off to the Tamil Eelam press accreditation tent.

Arya Rubesinghe's Department of Information press card is of absolutely no use around here. So I get this round bit of cardboard trailing gold and red ribbons to wear. A local Boy Scout troop stand impassively by, witnesses to my humiliation.

It was a hard morning on the playing fields of Trincomalee. Three hours of patriotic songs, stirring speeches and *Sieg Heils* for Eelam would be enough to exhaust anybody. Now I am ready for a nice cold beer . . . Unfortunately, it soon becomes apparent that the LTTE have given strict instructions. No beer today. I am not inclined to give up easily on this personal search for *nirvana* and so I set off on foot on the two kilometre walk (no three wheelers today, instructions of you know who) to the Seven Islands Hotel. Here I am furnished with a long cool glass of the amber nectar. Heaven.

That is until the arrival of Mr Chandrasekeran's convoy carrying the minister, various LTTE types and fellow travellers. They eye my beer disapprovingly and my request for a second is turned down by the hapless manager. "You know how it is around here," he moans pointing at the cadres lounging by the expensive four-wheel drives. "Please come back this evening," he adds brightly.

Mallavi is the brightest light in the firmament of the Vanni. It has a couple of LTTE hotels. At our modest little guest house I ask our LTTE minders to take us to a local night club. A peculiar pained expression crosses their visages. Of course, I am winding them up. I settled for a *kasippu* store and purchased a delicious bottle of arrack. But arrack is not approved of around here and the atmosphere is distinctly frosty as the cadres observe my alcoholic indulgence on the verandah as the sun goes down. I tell them I have a terminal illness and am required under doctors' orders to drink at least one bottle of spirits a day.

Shortly after 9 p.m. things rather deteriorate socially. I am more than half way down the bottle when the screeching of tyres announces visitors without an appointment. To be truthful I have observed some chaps skulking in the bushes with T-56 assault rifles but I have studiously ignored them, although they have persistently ruined the view through the bottom of my glass.

The gates open. A squad of goons – men in civvies and birds in ominous black uniforms – stalk up the drive. All except one, that is. He's on crutches so he's not in the stalking business any longer. He's a dude called Kokulan, LTTE security chief in charge of arrangements for Prabha's press conference. They've pitched up to "search baggage and examine equipment".

The operation lasted almost three hours. Cameras stripped down, minutely examined and photographed piece by piece. Photographic equipment weighed using a sensitive pair of scales, as was unexposed film and even a packet of biscuits in a search for plastic explosives. Serial numbers of all equipment taken and computers photographed. The operating systems checked out by a computer whizzkid. Me and my mate Bandula are very good humoured about all this. We keep up the jolly banter although our jokes seem to be falling a trifle flat.

As we are all gathering for the Big P's Address to the World, a well known Colombo photojournalist approaches. "Look, Paul, the

LTTE have asked me to ask you not to keep making fun of them."

I reacted without thinking. "You've got to be joking."

"No, please, no more jokes." And he scurried off back to the LTTE.

I give up. Welcome to Tamil Eelam. World Repository of Fun and Frolic. I don't think. Just pass me another beer. That reminds me. There isn't a single bottle of beer to be had *anywhere* in the uncleared areas. A good reason on its own not to be applying for citizenship papers for Tamil Eelam.

The *Lanka Monthly Digest* took out the reference to The Chief Genial Fatty: probably as well, I suppose. But the humour was hitting home much more effectively than I ever thought. That had, in retrospect, been an ominous run-in with the LTTE's security machine in April before Prabhakaran's press conference. I was singled out for a special three hour long search which involved stripping down and examining with digital and heat-seeking equipment my cameras and computer. I was, involuntarily, sharing a room with freelance journalist Bandula Jayasekera and he was unwittingly drawn into the net.

Maybe it had all started with my eulogy to the LTTE's devotion to the Austin Cambridge. Anyway, I wasn't playing the game according to the LTTE rulebook. But, as the only Western journalist living and working in Sri Lanka (apart from the BBC's Frances Harrison) I was really on my own; there was no rulebook so far as I was concerned.

Whilst my humour was hitting home, there were some serious developments taking place in the country. In May, I wrote for *Janes Intelligence Review* about the *de facto* division of the country: the article which so miffed the PM after he was given it by Nirj Deva. In another article I predicted the use of schoolchildren and other civilians in besieging and over running bases of the security forces. All these things came to pass and what seemed so shocking at the time became received wisdom within five or six months. I shared my intelligence and predictions at the end of May with the Ministry of Defence

– specifically with retired police chief Merrill Gooneratne who was now a Big Wheel there, a personal appointee of the PM. I got the impression my views and predictions were not taken seriously.

I had been asked to talk to MPs in a public room in parliament on May 9 after taking tea in the office of opposition leader Mahendra Rajapakse. In hindsight, that was probably a tactical mistake (talking, not the tea which had no after effects). More than 50 opposition MPs attended from the PA, the Marxist-oriented JVP and the Muslim NUA. The panel which sat with me at the top table included respected former Foreign Minister Lakshman Kadrigamar, a former President of the Oxford Union, Mahendra Rajapakse and Anura Bandaranaike, former Speaker of the House and son of the President. Not exactly a band of gangsters, I would muse bemusedly later. That afternoon a government minister, Rajitha Senaratne, dramatically announced that an M15 *(sic)* agent had been in parliament.

That evening I went to the European Union Birthday Party in the Hilton Hotel. After a few gins, this extraordinary fellow bounded up to me and announced, in the self-important way politicians do, that he had "exposed me in Parliament this afternoon as an M15 agent." I said I didn't have a clue who he was and he looked decidedly put out. Then I instructed him, "The M15 in Britain is a motorway, not a security organisation. Anyway, it's MI6 you will be meaning." He looked crushed. No sense of humour and I had made an enemy.

Three days later there was the fateful encounter with PM. This encounter was colourfully reported in the *Sunday Leader*. The newspaper I had come to edit now became my sternest critic with an editorial, gossip column items and 'inside' political pieces about me. Then the Directorate of Internal Intelligence started its work: surveillance started, my room was searched and hotel employees and records examined. Within two weeks the DII investigation had cleared me, although they discovered that my work visa had wrongly been made out by the clerk at immigration inscribing my designation 'BBC'. When I had pointed out the error, he shrugged his shoulders. "We put all resident British journalists in the BBC file." As there were only two British correspondents on the island with resident visas, it didn't seem that unreasonable. Who was I, newly arrived, to question the bureaucratic procedure?

After all the press comment, the senior and respected journalist, Gamini Werrakoon, editor of *The Island*, advised me. "You have been causing waves in this country," and, rattling the ice in his whisky at the Orient Club, he chuckled and added, "Tidal waves." The Orient Club is one of the most agreeable places in Colombo. A total anachronism in a decaying colonial mansion, the size of the spirits measures can always be relied upon. Gamini, one of the most interesting and agreeable chaps I would come across in Colombo, was a stalwart of the club and would drink there most evenings until the phone rang and his wife summoned him home.

When I was asked to write a weekly column in a local paper owned by the PM's uncle I construed it either as it as an attempt to rein me in, or as an arm's length conciliatory gesture. I met with Sujan Wijewardene at the Navratna Restaurant in the Taj Samudra. To be precise, we met in the closed and deserted grillroom next door, out of sight and ears of the curious. *The Daily Mirror* allowed me complete freedom. I wrote on all sorts of topics, again, usually in a light-hearted manner. Tongue in cheek, I praised the LTTE's police force who were strictly enforcing traffic discipline on their newly opened roads, in contrast to the island's recognised police force.

I was offered a job as editor of a planned new newspaper. The problem was it was to be backed by opposition PA stalwarts and it was to be associated with former media minister Mangala Samaraweera. The project was extensively discussed at a series of dinners at Mangala's home at Kotte, at Anura Bandaranaike's plush pad in Colombo 7's Rosmead

Place, and at the residences of other PA MPs. To me it would simply have been a professional assignment and I stipulated that I would brook no editorial interference from the owners or backers. But, after much consideration, I recognised the government would regard it as an inflammatory action if I took on the job, so I declined.

Nanda Godage phoned me at lunchtime on May 24. I was having lunch with a delightful Dutchman, long time resident – Permanent Guest – Hans Monhemius. Hans, along with Arthur C Clarke and Jim Spain, a retired US Ambassador to Sri Lanka, was one of three so-called Permanent Guests on the island. Hans had become an invaluable patron of the arts, energetically supporting music and the visual arts in Colombo.

Nanda told me that the National Intelligence Bureau investigation had turned up a problem. "People are saying you claimed to be a BBC correspondent in order to get your visa. The Prime Minister has been advised accordingly."

This was nonsense and I decided to deal with it immediately and wrote a letter that weekend, dated May 25, to the Foreign Ministry, addressed to Publicity Director Saj Mendis at the Ministry. It attempted to clarify, once and for all, my visa status. Events would prove that it had not and it is worth quoting in full:

I understand from the efficient Colombo 'grapevine' that the NIB investigation of myself is completed and has been lodged with the Prime Minister's office. I further understand that the colourful espionage rumours are now discounted. The report, apparently, finds only one problem in relation to my residency here and that is what has been adduced as representing a misdeclaration on my part, viz. my residency visa no. A/6714 enables me to engage in business or trade as a 'writer and journalist (BBC)' [photocopy attached].

When I attended at the Department of Immigration on November 21 last year I provided letter from *The Daily Telegraph* [photocopy attached] and filled in the form as representing *The*

Daily Telegraph. For reasoning known only to the department of Immigration, my visa was issued in the name of the BBC, with which body I have never claimed any connection whilst working here (I did work for the BBC in Slovenia, Croatia and Bosnia 1991-4). When I complained, it was shrugged off and I was told it was not important and I should not worry. At the time, I contacted Frances Harrison, BBC correspondent, in case it affected her position, but she said, "They put all British resident journalists in the BBC file. They've only got the one file."

This problem – not of my own making – seems to have come back to haunt me. Before the NIB's deductions occasion any unfortunate consequences – it would be unfortunate if I were to be deported on the day The Hon Ranil Wickremesinghe meets Prime Minister Tony Blair! – could you please contact Controller of Immigration Mr Bambarawanage and arrange for correction of their files and my passport visa?

Monday was a Poya Day holiday and I decided to go to the Foreign Ministry first thing the following morning with the letter for hand delivery. There I met with Saj Mendis while his assistant Rizvi Hassan hovered around in the background. The Foreign Ministry, in the person of Mendis, asked me not to say anything in public again, just to write. Director Saj Mendis suggested, for the first time, on the morning of Tuesday May 28 that my conduct could be construed as being prejudicial to national security. I thought he was just being pompous. Later I would realise that the seeds were already sown. I agreed not to speak again in public and subsequently turned down a string of invitations. I naively assumed the Foreign Ministry could be taken at is word and that peace had broken out.

I adopted a suitably low profile and moved out of the airy halls of the Galle Face Hotel after a Sinhala language Sunday paper, *Nawa Pereliya*, alleged my bills there were being paid by 'a conspiracy' of 'international arms dealers'. I was flattered to see the front page and two pages inside the paper devoted to me in its undated May issue.

It was headlined

ARMS DEALER PAUL HARRIS HELL BENT ON DESTROYING
PEACE HERE HAVING TALKS WITH WIMAL, DINESH
WIJITHAMUNI

It was not exactly a eulogy:

Paul Harris is an extremely dangerous person, whose job is
to go to war torn countries pretending to be a war reporter, deal
with terrorist organisations in his real capacity as an agent of arms
dealers and turn the war in to a 'beggar's wound' to the concerned
country. There are many instances where he has been involved
with reactionary terrorist groups in these countries, which include
Croatia, Bosnia, Sudan and Yugoslavia. It is easy for him to spark
off wars in these countries and all he need for this is the cover as
an international journalist.

It went on to affirm that I had met with opposition JVP
propaganda secretary Wimal Weerawansa (yes, once in the
street at a public demonstration!), and that 'he has assured
Weerawansa that he is able to get international help in the
form of arms, food and equipment to launch a fight against
the government.' As for the Dinesh character referred to in
the headline, I hadn't a clue who he was!

I thought it was laughable. Others were rather more
concerned. President's Council S L Gunesekera urged me to
sue *Nawa Pereliya*. I didn't see the point. Indeed, I felt that
litigation might lend the newspaper the credibility it did not
enjoy. But, most significantly, I learned the paper was owned by
the government minister who had lambasted me in Parliament
and tackled me at the EU party: Dr Rajitha Senaratne. An
unedifying character, I know him as Dr Death the Dentist.
In the late 1980s he headed up an organisation known as the
Pra Gang which was in the business of assassinating political
rivals. I would not have wanted my teeth drilled by this fellow
under any circumstances.

I took on, decorated and furnished a flat in the centre of

Colombo, just across the road from the Galle Face Hotel. I started a collection of the work of young local artists, took a course and learned the basics of the Sinhala language. My weekly column for *The Daily Mirror* seemed to be proving successful: I tried to take a wry, tangential look at events in Sri Lanka and many people were now buying the paper – just on the day my column was published ! My office must have had one of the best views in the world, out over the blue of the Indian Ocean over a panorama of coconut trees and urban bustle. I looked forward to settling down for many years in Sri Lanka and contemplated giving up unprofitable journalism in favour of making some investments in the country. I had also met a Chinese woman with whom I felt more comfortable and more attracted to than any other for a very long time.

I had met a wide variety of people in and around Colombo. Many had taken me into their confidence and into their lives. This gave me an extraordinary resource of material and experience for articles and columns. It is in the nature of things in Sri Lanka that the activities of those working against the current political system receive little coverage in the press and I was glad to be able to attempt to redress that balance.

I wrote in the *Daily Mirror* about the Sinhala support group, Success, whose dedicated, selfless work I much admired.

You don't hear much about Welioya in Colombo but physician and volunteer worker Dr Anula Wijesundere knows this remote part of the country well. It may not be marked on the maps but it occupies a strategic, triangular piece of land between Trincomaleee, Aanaradhapura and Mullativu. As she puts it, "This is the dreamland of the Tigers".

This patch of land, home to almost 10,000 isolated Sinhalese from just under 2,000 families, stands between Prabhakaran and his dream of a united north and east. The presence of these Sinhalese, in what is also their traditional homeland, is what stands in the way of the LTTE's dream of incorporating north and east in one mono-ethnic Tamil state.

The people of Welioya are simple, hardworking people used to backbreaking work in the fields or the hard life of the fisherman. There is no industry and very little in the way of infrastructure: medical facilities are almost non-existent for rural communities hereabouts and most services are provided by the army. There are no emergency services, virtually no police and little in the way of transport or education. This, it might be said, is Sri Lanka's lost tribe.

It was in Welioya that war first came to Sri Lankan civilians. On November 30 1984, the LTTE attacked the Kent and Dollor farms. In the ensuing massacre, 62 people died, mainly rehabilitated prisoners and their families.

Last weekend, I was privileged to join a team of 25 volunteers from the organisation Success working under Dr Anula Wijesundere. She qualified as a doctor in 1974 and has worked as a physician for the past twenty years. The volunteers who work with her in isolated Sinhala communities in the north and the east are a mix of retired consultants, junior doctors, pharmacists, paediatricians, nurses and social workers all bound together by a remarkable team spirit.

Last weekend they left Colombo at four in the morning on Saturday and returned in the early hours of Monday, many of them then going direct to their regular jobs, having snatched just a few hours sleep on the eight hour bus journey from Welioya.

During the past four years, this intrepid team has made more than fifty trips to the north and the east holding more than 150 clinics. Their work is carried out with the assistance of the Sri Lanka Army which identifies those people most in need and provides transport and logistics support.

The most common ailments encountered by the team include backache – from long hours in the fields; tension headaches; anaemia and thyroid deficiencies. At New Monaravela, Success distributed tools to local people as well as holding a clinic. The people came after the village of Monaravela, to the north, was attacked by the LTTE in November 1999. Now they have a village hall, built with the help of Success and the SLA. There is a bitterness evident. One villager opined, "We are forgotten. Even MSF and the ICRC don't come here. Just volunteers like Success and the army. Politicians don't come here except during elections. They make promises and disappear."

A retired consultant paediatrician said after the clinic, "of the children I have seen today, 80% are malnourished. They just get three meals a day of rice with no milk and no green vegetables."

There is little work around here for the people, just subsistence farming. The clinic in Sinhapura was well attended. More than 700 people, including 140 children, came from as far as 25 miles away – some on hired tractors - for a consultation with one of the six doctors. They were seen over a period of four hours. Another team distributed 93 pairs of spectacles to local people, returning to Colombo with just 17. One man, Mr U H Punjibanda, who acquired a pair of glasses, was pleased to show off his previous acquisition supplied by the team: an artificial leg jointed at the knee.

A local man at New Monoravela, who works as a teacher and local reporter, confirmed that people don't understand the intricacies of the MOU. "They are just happy that they no longer hear the sound of bombs and shooting. People fear that the war will start again. They find it difficult to believe the LTTE."

The last stop for the volunteers of Success was on Sunday evening as darkness fell at the village of Mahanikawela, near to Kabithygolowa. In this remote village the children were also seriously malnourished. Food, including lentils, noodles and dried milk, was distributed and then Dr Anula showed a side we had not seen previously that weekend as she launched into a ten minute admonitory lecture. The word *kasippu* featured large in the lecture as she sternly wagged her finger.

Afterwards she explained, "Despite their poverty – many of these people only earn a hundred rupees a day – they spend around half of their money on alcohol and cigarettes and don't feed their children."

The future is uncertain for all the peoples of Sri Lanka but one cannot help but feel that it is particularly fraught for those of remote Welioya. A return to war will snatch away from them the respite afforded by the MOU. A peace agreement might have even more devastating consequences. At worst, they face ethnic cleansing from their homes. At best, life as forgotten Sinhala people forced to live under an LTTE dominated administration with the support of the Sri Lanka Army removed.

As the bus makes its way back to Colombo in the dead of night, the volunteers who are not yet asleep sing the 1950s popular song *Kesera.*

Ke sera, sera
Whatever will be, will be
The future is not ours to see,
Ke sera, sera

The forthright attorney-at-law and sometime politician S L Gunesekera was a leading figure in Success. I regarded him as a true patriot in a country seemingly running rather short on them. His style is blunt, no nonsense – and why not when such an important matter as the future of your country is at stake? He published a book that summer entitled *The Wages of Sin* condemning LTTE atrocities. In the introduction to the book he took to task my critics, especially Rajitha Senaratne. 'Neither Senaratne nor the Sunday Leader sought to join issue with Harris about the merits of his opinions . . . (they were) cheap personal attacks'.

All this stuff, of course, was making me increasingly unpopular. After the altercation with the PM, surveillance and investigation had started. However, by the end of May I had the impression that the heat was off. The chap who had spent weeks underneath a coconut tree across the road from the hotel appeared to clear off.

However, as soon as I moved into Galle Face Court in July, the surveillance started again and my friend reappeared. Then he disappeared after a couple of weeks. I had started taking the back entrance to this building and used three wheelers driven by drivers unknown to me. It seems three wheeler drivers are an invaluable source of police information. I thought the pressure was off. Nanda urged me to live quietly and let the dust settle.

But, come October, the idyll was gradually shattered as the Foreign Ministry went silent. There was no response at all for permission sought by *The Daily Telegraph* to carry on my work. A September 30 letter signed by Alec Russell, the Foreign Editor, delivered by me by hand on October 7 was simply ignored. On personal visits to the Ministry nobody was available, although I spotted Nihal Rodrigo hovering furtively in the background. Nobody 'phoned back. Nobody wrote. A brick wall. When the surveillance restarted, I guessed that some sort of decision had probably been made but I was being left in the dark. But friends and fellow journalists were being given startling information. I was "a threat to national security".

On the morning of October 25, I went to the Peace Secretariat to see Nanda Godage who was working there in an unspecified new role. He lifted the telephone and called the acting Secretary at the Foreign Ministry. Both Secretary Nihal Rodrigo and Minister Fernando were abroad in China and Indonesia respectively. Acting Secretary Navratnarajah, Rodrigo's deputy honcho, jovially confided to Godage that my visa would not be renewed. Evidently, "a matter of national security" and, quoth he, "it's political". Nanda pointed out the implications . . . but it was clear that the matter was being dealt with at a rather higher level than the Foreign Ministry.

I called upon the British High Commission with just over a week to go. The Deputy High Commissioner, Mr Peter Hughes, was urbane and charming in the manner of the British diplomatic service. He assured me that the British government disapproved of the suppression of free speech and would energetically take up my case. "You'll find it's not that easy for them to throw out a British journalist." Splendid stuff, just what I wanted to hear, old boy. With eight days to go, pressure would be applied after the following Monday's holiday.

When information emerged, via my own links with the Sri Lankan intelligence services, about LTTE involvement in the decision to make me leave, I conveyed this personally to the High Commissioner, Stephen Evans, recently arrived in the posting after having served in Afghanistan in the wake of the fall of the Taliban. He cautiously agreed that, from the information he had, it "seemed likely" that accommodating the LTTE was a factor in the government's decision to have me removed from the scene.

Both The High Commissioner and his Deputy had arrived in Sri Lanka in the last few months. Both were patient and courteous. Evans is a former Sandhurst cadet and the manners to go with the territory. I guess they were also exceedingly patient with the Sri Lankan authorities. The Foreign Ministry did not return any of their calls, until the night before my visa expired. In truth, I suspect the British High Commission did not try very hard on my behalf. It is a naïve fallacy to believe that diplomatic missions abroad exist to help out citizens who have got themselves into scrapes. Rather, they exist to promote good relations with the ruling government in whichever country they are located; whether the government there be made up of very nice people or brutal sexual deviants, murderers and torturers. Making the best of a bad job for HMG, old boy.

With three days to go, on Wednesday November 6, I appealed to the President, Mrs Chandrika Bandaranaike Kumaratunga. Much maligned in the local press, I have always found her a brisk, no-nonsense lady of charm and presence. Fools are not suffered gladly and she uses her tongue scathingly on those who try to put one past her. She is the sort of woman I can deal with. She reminds me of Margaret Thatcher in her political prime.

Her press spokesman Harim Pieris picked me up in his car on the edge of Galle Face Green, just across the road from my apartment. I walked over to await him and deliberately placed myself beside two characters who had been lounging underneath a *palmyrah* tree since shortly after 8 a.m. I greeted them cordially. "Good morning, gentlemen." One wearing a flowing white shirt and black trousers and sporting the obligatory bulge of an automatic pistol smiled wanly at me.

The President saw me in her office overlooking the lawn immediately upon arrival at President's House. I only waited five minutes to see her. Any Sri Lankan will appreciate quite how remarkable that was.

Her office is more like something from an English country house rather than South Asia: the windows give onto neatly manicured lawns, family photographs adorn desk and sideboard and a fine 19th century oil painting is the central feature of the room. The largest among the family photographs is that of her late husband: murdered by the LTTE. The oil painting, stolen from President's House by an unscrupulous politician was recovered in the nick of time from a London auction house as it was about to go under the hammer a few years ago.

Mrs Kumaratunga gave every appearance of genuine concern. She had previously asked to see me to discuss the security situation in the country. She then told me that the commander in chief of the army had given her my article from the May issue of *Jane's Intelligence Review*. As she is constitutionally the commander of the armed forces, I could see no threat to national security in this. Quite the opposite, indeed.

The President duly rattled the bars on the cages in the Foreign Ministry but even she could not extract the necessary paperwork. However, one of the real highlights of my long sojourn in Sri Lanka must have been having the privilege of hearing President Kumaratunga roundly admonishing the aforementioned Rodrigo for his duplicity in the matter of my visa. As the poor fellow wriggled and squirmed, producing one feeble reason after another for its non-renewal, Madam weighed in mercilessly like the street fighter she is, roundly admonishing the hapless fellow. The President explained to me that she had no power to grant a visa to me: that power, apparently, lay with the Minister of Defence, and she had given up her role in that Ministry. One of the president's close associates, however, assured me that as soon as the government changed I would be welcomed back to the country. "Military band on the tarmac at the airport." [In fact, my couriered correspondence to the President would go unanswered in the spring of 2004 after the PA regained power.]

The Foreign Ministry at no stage contacted me or explained the situation. Meantime, they did find time to tip off the island gossip, Bandula Jayasekera, who was then working for the website Lanka Academic. However, when Bandula called me to ask if it was true that I was being denied a visa to stay, I could, in all honesty, tell him that I had not heard that. With a day to go, I attended the weekly cabinet press briefing. I publicly asked Cabinet press spokesman and Minister for Constitutional Affairs G L Pieris, what was happening and if he could guarantee my security. My query did not bear fruit – but at least, in my final hour, it made my predicament clear before an audience of journalists. Bespectacled, earnest Pieris, a man with a permanent air of being from some other world, looked puzzled, said he knew nothing, and said he certainly could not guarantee my safety. "I cannot and I will not," he observed in a rather final manner.

Predictably, I was then tackled by several local journalists at the end of the press conference. I went public on what was happening with just 36 hours to go.

That afternoon, the President told the nation, "The President's Office takes serious note of the government's decision not to extend the visa of journalist Mr Paul Harris . . . The President's Office recalls that Mr Harris had accurately at the start of this year predicted certain developments with regard to the LTTE in the peace process: specifically, the use of schoolchildren and civilians to storm security forces' camps. Further, we recognise that Mr Harris has freely reported on matters potentially embarrassing to the government and definitely embarrassing to the LTTE, namely the human rights violations in the north and the east subsequent to the ceasefire MOU, specifically that of child conscription, extortion and security issues of the Muslim community in the East. Freedom of expression and the right of dissent are bedrock requirements for a democratic and free society and this insidious silencing of an often lone voice against the conventional wisdom of the government is a serious erosion of media freedom and a setback for democracy in Sri Lanka . . . The President has received no valid or acceptable reason from the Foreign Ministry for refusing to extend Mr Harris's visa and has informed the Government that it is not correct to refuse a visa for a journalist from a friendly country who has done no wrong."

The next morning the telephone started to ring at 6.30. One newspaper carried the front page headline 'British journalist forced to leave Lanka'. *The Island* newspaper also headed its editorial for my last day, Friday, Hands off Paul Harris. I was moved by its support, "Mr Paul Harris undoubtedly is not a run-of-the-mill foreign correspondent. He has exposed LTTE violations of basic human rights in areas under LTTE control and brilliantly exposed the fascist nature of LTTE with the photograph of thousands of LTTE cadres delivering the fascist Hitlerite salute to LTTE leaders." Thanks, Gamini.

Nanda made one of the dozens of telephone calls which came in. "What you have never understood about this country, Paul, is that it is based on rumour, not humour."

With 24 hours to go I had to make the decision to buy the air tickets out. I poured a glass of treasured Laphroaig whisky, from faraway Islay, and surveyed my apartment: the paintings on the wall, the framed photographs, the visitors' book filled at my housewarming party with all the good wishes for the future. Of course, I felt sorry for myself. It was difficult to make the decisions about what to leave and what to take. I packed and unpacked the suitcase. Does the practical value of an electric shaver outweigh the emotional value of a family photograph? Fine as an academic question in a moral philosophy examination, but remarkably difficult to determine in real life.

Of course, it could be said I should have made contingency plans; seen this coming. But, like the insouciant peasant in a dozen wars I had covered, I hung on within the security afforded by the four walls we call home and assumed things would work out and nothing would impinge on it. At least I was getting away with my life ...

I left with three and a half hours to go on my visa with just one suitcase, some hand baggage ... and my girlfriend. The press were waiting outside and I didn't take too much notice of everybody hanging around by the door. However, my driver, himself a former policeman, sent by a local businessman to transport me to the airport, said he recognised several characters lurking in the street as CID officers. There was no time to protect my investments, organise my property, sell my especially hand-made furniture or extract money in local non-negotiable currency in my bank accounts.

Maybe I was naïve to expect better things but I kept saying to myself, "This is not Zimbabwe, this is Sri Lanka.". I suppose I was quite wrong.

When I left the country, with four hours left on my visa, there was still no response to me, or *The Telegraph*, or the British High Commission, from the Foreign Ministry. But, even as I left, the media were being given a ludicrous list of my alleged visa infractions: arriving on a tourist visa, writing articles for the local newspaper *The Daily Mirror*, making unfounded allegations of surveillance by armed men, and they said that it had just come to their attention, via a press release from the president, that I worked for *Jane's Intelligence Review*. "This disclosure only confirms the decision of the government not to renew Mr Harris's visa ...". Oh dear, back to that espionage red herring ...

A local businessman, who I did not know that well, had taken the trouble to telephone shortly after 6.30 that morning. He professed to be 'ashamed' of his country, and kindly sent his air-conditioned Mercedes. "This is an appalling injustice but at least you will leave in style." Such small kindnesses are moving when you feel isolated and rejected. As I left the building where I lived, the security staff, three- wheeler drivers and local shopkeepers all lined up and shook my hand. Ordinary people, not your politicians or urban sophisticates. One simply said to me, "We know you told the truth."

I then knew I had done the right thing. The cost has been severe. The hurt and disappointment was great. What the future might hold, I hadn't a clue. And, I thought, it's a pity I shall not be able to use my Sinhala for a while, maybe not ever again.

At Colombo's Bandaranaike Airport, a television crew was waiting. I told them that I loved Sri Lanka and hoped that I would be able to return. The immigration officer who checked us out, with four hours left on my visa, immediately recognised me. "I read all your articles," he cheerily observed as he stamped the exit visa. "You know what's *really* happening here."

***

I flew with my Chinese girlfriend, Sulee, to Male Airport in The Maldives. This 1,200 island archipelago is just over an hour's flying from Colombo but a world away in so many respects. The Maldives are organised, prosperous and safe. Arrival at the airport reminds me of Venice rather than the southern Indian Ocean. Once clear of immigration and customs we are met by a representative of Universal Resorts and whisked to a motor launch tied up at the airport quayside. No broken, crowded roads to battle. No importuning touts, bagmen or taxi drivers to fight off.

Transport is either by fast launch to the nearer islands; otherwise by modern seaplane. Currently, there are 96 resort islands and more are under development. As only 200 of the islands of the Maldives are inhabited, there is still enormous potential for development.

It is but six or seven minutes to Kurumba Village, the very first resort developed in The Maldives in 1970. We stay there for six nights as the guest of Mr Mohamed Maniku, the Chairman of Universal. I had met him the previous July in

Colombo when I spoke at – and gave away the prizes – at the annual prize-giving of the British School in Colombo, held in the ballroom of the GFH. I attended the event with some trepidation: the Ministry of Foreign Affairs having told me not to speak in public again. But, I thought, what harm could there be in addressing a few hundred schoolchildren with some words about making the best of their future? But it was probably another nail in my coffin, so to speak.

Afterwards, when I confessed to the Chairman of the school – Mr Mohamed Maniku – that I had never visited The Maldives, he promptly invited me to visit as his guest. The constant demands on a journalist who must ever be available to cover any news that might break debarred me from immediately taking up his offer but the uncertainty over my visa and future gave me that window of opportunity to take him up on his generous offer.

After Kurumba, Mr Maniku moved us for three days at Full Moon Beach, an exclusive, intimate resort island. What could be more perfect? From the private sundeck of our sea bungalow at the exclusive resort of Full Moon, just fifteen minutes or so by speedboat from Male Airport, the sea stretches out to the reef beyond in strips of blue and turquoise green. We have soon opened the complimentary bottle of Bourgogne Grand Ordinaire and are tucking into the bowl of delicious fresh fruit: a piece of papaya drops into the translucent water and a dozen multi-coloured fish pounce on the morsel.

The contrast between the 1,200 island archipelago of The Maldives and the single island of Sri Lanka is startling, particularly at this time, and considering the two countries are just over an hour's flying away from each other.

Each resort island has its own characteristics: its own range of water-sports and aquatic activities, its own architecture and layout, its own individual style. Whereas Kurumba Village was a large bustling resort with every imaginable facility, a range of international restaurants and a clientele drawn from all over the world, including the UK, Germany, Italy, Russia, Korea and Japan. ll the staff from desk clerks to chefs seem well aware of the requirements of guests of different nationalities. On a breakfast table there is even that great British 'delicacy' HP Sauce.

Kurumba is a Universal resort and is still, for Chairman Mr Maniku, the apple of his eye. It has recently had a complete overhaul of all public areas and the rebuilding of much of the accommodation in the secluded, private bungalow style increasingly favoured by visitors seeking personal privacy and seclusion. As one of his managers puts it, "We are doing well now but we cannot rest or we might have a problem staying in the market. So we look ahead all the time."

Full Moon is another Universal resort just six minutes away by launch but a world away in style. It was created by Universal in just nine months although you would never guess that was so. Smaller in size and with a more intimate atmosphere, it somehow feels as if it is a more authentic Maldivian experience. That is, of course, a cleverly achieved illusion: a fulfilment of a Western dream of carefree life on a desert island. As you step into your water bungalow with its endless vista of blue sky and ocean the realities of everyday life are suspended.

There are 52 water bungalows and these are the 'hot sellers' in the 156-room resort. Says deputy manager Mohamed Mumthaz, an Indian like so many of the managerial professionals here, "Today people want more privacy." Foreign tour operators like the British upmarket Kuoni operation snap up the water bungalows for their clients, despite the US$300 a night price tag – food and beverages extra. That is a hefty price for a UK tour operator to pay but they are clearly impressed by the quality of the product.

And if you want to go further up market, fifteen minutes boat ride away is the exclusive four year-old Four Seasons Resort where you will have to fork out US$12-1400 a night for a de-luxe water bungalow with its own sitting room and two bathrooms; or you can get a cheaper beach bungalow for a mere $800 a night! When I was there, Four Seasons was 100% sold out at these sky high rates aimed at the seriously rich.

For the overseas visitor this destination is synonymous with style, comfort and an exotic experience. This is a triumph of marketing and developers will tell you that it has been achieved over the last decade as a direct result of strategic development. The success of The Maldives is a carefully nurtured one: it is not based on a series of accidental discoveries and there is much for a reviving Sri Lankan tourist industry to learn here. The Maldivians have become accomplished at engineering a dream machine. The expectations of guests are spectacularly fulfilled. The Universal resort of Baros – another small, intimate island – boasts between 60 and 80% 'repeaters' during high season: a staggering tangible endorsement of its success.

Although The Maldives is a strict Muslim country, the resorts are free of any impositions of Islamic law or culture. The visitors' holidays are not interrupted by compulsory alcohol free holidays: unlike the Poya Day problems of Sri Lanka or World Temperance Day, so scrupulously observed at the GFH. There is the best, coldest beer I have tasted anywhere in Asia. Even in Colombo, I have experienced difficulty getting an ice cold, preferably draught, beer. A Sri Lankan manager at a resort island shakes his head and observes, "Over the last twenty years the Sri Lankan hotel industry has not had enough foreign visitors and standards have slipped." The beaches are spotlessly clean and that great curse of Sri Lanka, personal litter, is not to be seen anywhere.

The remote nature of the Maldivian experience, allied to a greater affluence in the general population, means that one of the greatest detractions of Sri Lanka for the tourist are absent here. There is no harassment, no importuning trishaw drivers, no imprecations to buy, 'be my friend', or subscribe to school improvement schemes. The absence of this sort of unwelcome pressure is, I reflect, vital to the establishment of a firmly based tourist industry.

After ten days in The Maldives, we decided to return to Sri Lanka in the early hours of Sunday morning. Just before dawn is, as all strategists know, the optimum time for attack. The alertness of your enemies is at its lowest ebb. The plane touched down just before 3 a.m. Most of the passengers were European tourists in transit on the way home. The lines were short and the immigration officers tired and bored. I positioned myself behind some foreigner of indeterminate origin and my Chinese girlfriend was behind me. The chap in front got a thorough check but mine was cursory; not even that. The immigration officer did not even look at the passport. He simply opened it and stamped it with a 30 day tourist visa, pushing the landing card to one side as he stared around with studied boredom.

I recognised him. He was the immigration chap who had told me on the way out, "You are the only person in this country who knows what is going on. Here (at the airport) we read all your articles."

Sulee got the third degree. Her passport was minutely examined and the many entry and exit stamps perused; questions about her educational status; eventually, an entry stamp with no further days granted. She had three days left on her previous visa ...

Colombo was deserted and the taxi sped in on the airport road. When we arrived at Galle Face Court, street and parking lot were deserted, even the security men were asleep. I was relieved when the door was opened by a security guard I did not know. He did not appear to recognise me, either. We left the blinds down in the deserted flat, not even raising them with daylight as dawn broke. Surveillance had clearly been lifted but we decided it was best not to be seen by anybody looking up from the street. The telephone rang a few times on Sunday but we ignored it. Sulee went out for newspapers but otherwise we remained indoors. *The Sunday Times* carried on page two the text of a statement about me by Prime Minister Wickremesinghe. 'PM says Paul Harris violated visa regulations'.

The Prime Minister's office had clearly released the text of the PM's letter written in reply to a complaint from the Editors' Guild of Sri Lanka. His response made it clear that I had been thrown out for my journalism: specifically, for writing the column for *The Daily Mirror*. The PM admitted to ambiguity in the visa regulations – and said that they would be clarified in future – but, apparently, foreign journalists were debarred from writing for local media. He declined the Editors' Guild request for an opportunity for me to present my case in my defence as this would establish a precedent. The PM's statement was, in a way, a relief. He had confirmed that I was ejected for my writing which left me with a degree of honour which would have been stripped away if some other, extraneous allegation of misconduct had been made.

On Monday morning, I decided to pay a visit to the British High Commission, just a few hundred metres down the road. The tenuous nature of my presence in the country, and the requirement to attempt to get a UK visa for Sulee, required such a visit. I gingerly made my way out of the building, abjuring use of the lift and sneaking around the back of the lift shaft and out through the rubbish yard at the back.

Peter Hughes, the deputy High Commissioner, was visibly surprised, if not downright astonished, to see me back. He accepted my explanation that I had to return in an attempt to clear up personal and business matters but was clearly uneasy about it. I expressed my disappointment at the ineffective nature of the protests lodged by the representatives of Her Majesty's government. Hughes made his excuses: the whole matter was quite irreversible. "Everything to do with your situation is being dealt with at Temple Trees across the road." He nodded out of his window to the landscaped grounds of the PM's official residence, just a hundred metres away. All approaches to the Foreign Ministry which the BHC had made had been futile. It was being dealt with at a rather higher level, he confirmed. And it become personal.

The BHC was clearly uneasy about my return as a tourist with all its potential for even more drama. I assured Hughes that I would maintain a low profile, not contact the media, keep the blinds fully down – literally and metaphorically, and clear off just as soon as I had things wrapped up. Oh, and could I please have a visa for my girlfriend to go back with me to the UK?

Oh, yes, we'll see about that. What passport? China? PRC? Gulp. But within three hours the visa was issued . . . and I solemnly undertook to remove myself as soon as possible from the scene.

In the waiting room downstairs, the local BHC 'information officer' Mahendra Ratnaweera greeted me. He was evidently as surprised as Hughes to see me back. Seeing him was not good news. Well connected to the Colombo grapevine, and a close friend of Bandula Jayasekera, a freelance journo and incorrigible local gossip working closely with the Lanka Academic news website and the TNL Newsroom.

The evening TNL TV News duly announced that Paul Harris was back . . . even my visa details were disclosed.

Of course, the next day the surveillance restarted . . .

Taking a roundabout route, that afternoon I visited a 'friendly' member of the Sri Lankan intelligence community. He brought me up to date. Yes, it was personal with the PM and he had put his personal Prime Ministerial security people on the job using a unit specially established within Temple Trees, his official residence, but there was rather more to it. The LTTE had, apparently, become incensed over my journalism and had demanded of the PM's office that I be removed from the scene. They had advised that otherwise there would be consequences for the peace process! Anyway if I was not removed from the scene, they would do it themselves . . . He advised me to leave Colombo immediately otherwise there would probably be an accident. Nothing dramatic like assassination. "You'll just get run over crossing the road. Something everyday like that."

That evening a friend who was Second Secretary in a European Embassy came around for a drink. He simply confirmed what I now knew. No wonder the people at the British High Commission had been so nervous about my presence. They must have been party to information that was common currency on the diplomatic network.

Sulee and I left Colombo and went to a hotel lurking behind a walled enclosure in the very south of the island. The Horizon Hotel was a welcome retreat from the hothouse atmosphere of Colombo. But, after a couple of nights in residence, the local police took to dining at the next table to us. The time had really come to move on and I ordered a taxi from Colombo to take us to the airport.

At the airport, four hours later, I made to pay the bill but my money was refused by the driver. He handed me a note from his boss thanking me for my work for Sri Lanka and we presented ourselves at the London check-in counter.

* * *

In *The Sunday Times* on January 11 2003 columnist Gaston de Rosayro – a commentator unknown to me, I might make it clear – commented on the business of my expulsion.

The extraordinary lengths to which the administration went to send journalist Paul Harris packing has done more to discredit government policy on its much touted new democratic culture and press freedom than anything else. It has also given allowance for widespread speculation that Harris' deportation was triggered by the demands of a piqued Tiger hierarchy to which the kow-towing Government so readily obliged.

Paul Harris is an intelligent, dogged and deftly analytical journalist. He has proved himself sharper and more professional than anyone the politicized Government propaganda machine has hired.

Forcing him to leave on pathetic excuses of his having flouted the immigration laws of this country was neither a strategic nor sensible move. All the world wants is a dose of plain truth and Harris it appears was getting to close to it for the comfort of certain parties.

Thank you, Gaston. Enough said . . .

Reception ballroom

Bibliography

Adamson, Peter *Facing Out to Sea* London 1997

Brohier, Deloraine *The Saga of the Colombo Club* Colombo 2001

Cambrai, Jeanne *Murder in the Pettah* New Delhi 2001

Carpenter, Mary Thorn *A Girl's Winter in India* New York 1892

Coward, Noel *Present Indicative* New York 1937

Darling, Harold *Bon Voyage! Souvenirs from the Golden Age of Travel* New York 1990

Foster, Harry *A Beachcomber in the Orient* New York 1923

Gunesekera, S L *The Wages of Sin* Colombo 2002

Harris, Paul *Fractured Paradise: Images of Sri Lanka* Colombo & Edinburgh 2001

Hulugalle, H A J *Centenary Volume of the Colombo Municipal Council 1865-1965* Colombo 1965

Keyes, Francis Parkinson *Coral Strands* New York 1926

Lear, Edward *Edward Lear's Indian Journal* London n.d.

Malraux, Andre *Antememoirs* London 1968

Moraes, Premnath *Once Upon an Island* Colombo 1993

Morley, Sheridan *A Talent to Amuse: a Biography of Noel Coward* Boston 1969

Muller, Carl *Colombo A Novel* New Delhi 1995

Ondaatje, Christopher *The Man-Eater of Punanai* Toronto 1992

Rogers, Clara Kathleen *Journal-Letters from the Orient* ed. H M Rogers, Massachusetts 1934

Twain, Mark *Following the Equator: A Journey Around the World* London 1900

Twentieth Century Impressions of Ceylon, London 1907

Seaports of the Far East 1913

Present Day Impressions of the Far East 1917

The files of ANCL, Lake House, Colombo

Afterword

*Following his expulsion from Sri Lanka, in January 2003 Paul Harris was invited to Shanghai as a foreign expert with the Chinese press working on **The Shanghai Daily** newspaper. On August 28 2003, in Shenyang, China, he married Sulee, the Chinese woman he met in Sri Lanka and who fled the country with him. On August 3 2004 their daughter, Lucy, was born in Shanghai.*

On November 1 2004, they went to live in Scotland. On November 19 2004 representatives of the British security service MI5 advised Paul Harris that there was 'a directive' issued by the LTTE ordering his assassination. The threat was urgent and he was immediately put under 24 hour armed guard by MI5. On a brief 48 hour visit to speak in public in Sri Lanka in December 2004 he was assigned MSD protection (Ministerial Security Detail) and thereafter lived in the UK under armed protection until relocating secretly the following year to another island state friendly to the British government.

During 2005, the ceasefire in Sri Lanka was repeatedly and flagrantly broken by the LTTE, culminating in the assassination by a sniper of the country's Foreign Minister Lakshman Kadrigamar on August 12 as he was getting out of the swimming pool at his residence in Colombo. Kadrigamar, himself a Tamil, was probably the most respected Sri Lankan politician of the 20th century.

During 2006, the ceasefire existed only in name with widespread attacks on the Sri Lanka army and, even, Army Headquarters and generals in Colombo. The LTTE has also utilised the period of the ceasefire to eradicate political opposition and journalists. As in its entire operational history, the LTTE has never admitted to any of these attacks although, in June 2006, the European Union passed its own judgement and outlawed the LTTE as terrorists. The LTTE now controls most of the land mass of Sri Lanka.

Paul Harris feels totally vindicated in the firm stand he took, and continues to take, against the LTTE.

Index of People

View to fort

Printed in the United Kingdom
by Lightning Source UK Ltd.
115905UKS00001BA/13-18